Praise Avenue

DON GOSSETT

WHITAKER
HOUSE

All Scripture quotations are taken from the King James Version of the Holy Bible.

Praise Avenue

Don Gossett
P.O. Box 2
Blaine, Washington 98231
www.dongossett.com

IBSN: 978-1-60374-701-1
eBook ISBN: 978-1-60374-702-8
Printed in the United States of America
© 1976, 2012 by Don Gossett

Whitaker House
1030 Hunt Valley Circle
New Kensington, PA 15068
www.whitakerhouse.com

This book has been printed digitally and produced in a standard specification in order to ensure its continuing availability.

There are two kinds of people in the world: those who are in pursuit of happiness and those who have caught up with it.

In this age of computers, the Internet, calamity, and terrorism, you need more than just a theory to survive the tensions.

Take a look at the easy-to-understand instructions in this book. Then give them an honest try. You'll find that happiness is easier than you think!

CONTENTS

FOREWORD BY ANDRAE CROUCH

As I travel to different parts of the world, I meet many people who take a very negative view of life—people who complain and grumble over their misfortunes—people who dream of where they could have been if there hadn't been trials and hard times.

Frankly, I find myself wondering how many of them might have reached far greater heights had they learned how to rise up over their defeats through praise. The secret is simple, and there's something uplifting about praising and rejoicing "through it all."

Don Gossett is a real brother and a man of faith whom we love and appreciate. His message has been a great inspiration to millions around the world. He gets to the bottom of the secrets of praise in this book.

As Don Gossett shares his experiences and what he has learned about the powerful practice of praising, you too will see signs and landmarks directing you to *Praise Avenue*.

Now sit back and enjoy this book. Remember, in all things, keep praising! That's the secret!

ONE

DON'T PANIC—PRAISE!

Hurled from the car, I smashed into a snow bank and felt more than two tons of automobile rolling over me.

Weakly, I gasped out the words, "Lord, help me! Don't let me die!"

Then, from somewhere, came the strong impression: *But you're not going to die.*

"Not going to die?" I thought. "Better to die than to be crippled for life."

Slowly and painfully pulling myself from the snow bank, I was amazed that I could stand. As I stood there looking at the car that had rolled farther down the hill, I began to feel my body for broken bones. I rubbed my hands over my face and neck, looking for signs of blood.

There was none!

Just then, a group of highway workmen came rushing toward me. They were shocked to see me standing there alive, let alone uninjured—especially since the accident demolished my aging Buick.

"Nuthin' but pure luck!" one of the men exclaimed. "Do you realize that car rolled right over top of you? You oughta be dead!"

With as much of a smile as I could muster, I told them that it wasn't luck that pulled me through, but the Lord who protected me.

Little by little, I began grasping that fact more and more. God—that great big God—was taking care of me—Don Gossett! Seeing that clearly, I decided there was no point in worrying about anything. If God was looking after me, then I should praise Him in every situation.

Through the years, that conviction grew. I've been in all kinds of situations that weren't very conducive to praising God. But I've become so convinced about the power of praise that very few things upset me anymore.

Sometime after the first wreck, for instance, I had another serious accident while en route to Chicago. This time I noticed how natural praising God had become. As my car slid off the highway and rolled end over end, my helpless body was tossed from the front seat into the back seat. When the car stopped rolling, it turned out that I was trapped inside. The cold trickle of gasoline was running over my body. I could smell the pungent fumes as I lay there pinned in the wreckage. Immediately, though, the Holy Spirit reminded me to offer up praises to God. Fully confident that God was in control of that situation, I obeyed.

Lying there quietly praising the Lord, I heard a man outside the car say, "We better get that guy out fast! That gas could ignite any minute and burn him alive!"

It might sound strange to some people, but I can honestly say that I wasn't worried. Knowing the Lord would preserve me, I just lay back and waited patiently for the men to pry the wreckage open so that I could get out.

When they finally got me out, all I could do was stand there and thank God for His mighty protection.

Scores of people stopped their cars on that busy highway. When they saw how that Oldsmobile was smashed and battered, they asked, "Who got killed?" "Who was in it?"

Each time, I would step up to them and say, "I'm the one who was in that car. The Lord kept His hand on me, and here I stand." I don't think I've seen so many surprised faces in all my life before or since then.

"But can praise really change things?" you ask. Some years back, I would never have thought of that question—let alone successfully answered it. Yet, through the years, and time after time, I have found that praise really works miracles.

I am not alone in this discovery. Reginald Layzell was a successful sales manager for a large office supplies company in Toronto, Ontario, when he went west for a series of speaking engagements at a church in Abbotsford, British Columbia. Although prominent in business, Reg often took time to do lay preaching.

Reg tried hard, but the first talks seemed to fall on deaf ears. Admitting that his meetings were a failure, Reg resorted to prayer and fasting. When that didn't seem to help, he considered the idea of closing his meetings and going home.

On the first day of prayer, however, something happened. He was reminded of a passage in the Psalms. He didn't know it was Psalm 22:3, but the words of the verse were brought to his memory by the Holy Spirit, and he knew that he read it before: *"But thou art holy. O thou that inhabitest the praises of Israel."*

At first, Reg thought only about the first part of the verse—about how holy God is. But then the Holy Spirit led him on to the second half of the verse, where the Psalmist refers to God as the one *"who inhabitest the praises of Israel."* Suddenly, the heavens seemed to open, and the full impact of that verse emblazoned itself upon his mind: God actually lives in the praises of His people!

This was a revolutionary thought. Even though God is high and lifted up, He will actually dwell (and manifest Himself) where praise ascends to Him! The thoughts tumbled through Reg's mind in rapid succession: "If He dwells in praise, then the thing I must do is fill this building with praise, and God will come down and live in it."

Reg decided to take action. If his thought was from God, then it would work; if not, he would find out quickly enough. Since he was such a dismal failure, he had nothing to lose. And he had everything to gain if it was true.

So, in simple obedience to the Word of God, and with implicit faith in the teaching of that verse, he began praising the Lord, even though he felt depressed and discouraged.

Fortunately, he was alone; otherwise the embarrassment of raising his hands and praising God aloud might have been too much to bear. This was especially true since his entire nature and background were diametrically opposed to this type of practice; he was a composed, staid, solemn Englishman.

After a session of praise in a small study room, he ventured into the church. "I certainly need God at the pulpit," he admitted, "so I'll go up there and praise the Lord." And that is just what he did.

After that, he said, "The pianist is rather dead too," so he went around and around the piano with praises, trusting God to come down and dwell there also.

Up and down each aisle, in and out between the pews, downstairs into every room (including the washrooms) he went, praising God constantly.

The hours of the afternoon rolled by, yet he still walked through the building, audibly praising God. With each passing hour, self-consciousness lessened and the praises grew louder. Supper hour came and went unheeded; the praises continued.

It had been a deliberate decision to act by sheer, raw faith, absolutely devoid of any feelings. He knew only one thing: God's

Word said that He would dwell in praise, and He was going to "put it to the test."

About seven o'clock, others started arriving at the church to pray before the service; Reg knelt at the altar and praised the Lord a little longer.

A few minutes later, he began the service with the singing of the hymn, "There is Power in the Blood." They had sung only the first verse when all of a sudden a woman lifted her hands to God in praise, and was mightily baptized in the Holy Spirit. From that moment, the revival was on.

To some, it might seem incredible that such a transition from abject failure to glorious revival could take place through the revelation of one verse of Scripture. But miracles are bound to happen when anyone really believes the Word of God.

Reg, who later became founder and pastor of Glad Tidings Temple, one of the greatest churches in the Canadian West, explains his convictions about praise this way:

> On more than one occasion, I have said that if I should be limited to one subject in my preaching, I would choose, without hesitation, the subject of praising Jesus. This would be for various reasons.

> First, I owe everything to Jesus and His mercy. If it were not for Jesus, I would still be in my sins and lost. I am sure that, but for Jesus, I would be dead and in hell. Jesus did everything for me and I can't praise Him too much.

> I also find that the Word of God, which is our guide to life, tells us to praise Him in many things and at all times. There are probably more passages on praise and worship in the Bible than on any other single subject.

> I have found that in the preaching and practicing of praising Jesus, every avenue of the Gospel is effective. Jesus

inhabits the praises of Israel. Because He is present in the atmosphere of true Bible praise, sinners are saved, people are healed, believers are baptized in the Holy Spirit, and all are blessed.

Such is the power of praise. And after I read Reg Layzell's comments on the subject, my mind went back to a prayer meeting I attended when God was teaching me some early lessons on praise. During the meeting, a gentleman stood up and started to recite a long list of trials, tribulations, woes, and troubles which he was encountering on the way to heaven. I couldn't have sympathized with him more as I sat there and listened.

After this gentleman sat down, another stood up and said, "I see that our friend here is living on Grumbling Street. Every day of life there is a struggle. I used to live on Grumbling Street too." He went on to explain how gloomy his life used to be: how poor his health, how joyless his outlook, how depressed his mentality. "But finally, I moved onto Praise Avenue," he said with a grin. "And ever since that move, I've had a lot more sunshine, the air is better—even my health improved!"

I was deeply stirred, and disturbed at the same time, because I recognized that I was sometimes like the first man who was living on Grumbling Street.

How much of my life was spent in praising God, compared to the times spent in fruitless expression of discontent? I was ashamed to admit that I gave more of my time to worrying than to praising my Creator.

As I mulled over these things on my way home, I thought about the Hebrews as they traveled through the wilderness with Moses. There was a multitude of people whom God delivered from bondage in Egypt. He parted the Red Sea for their escape; He miraculously fed them with manna. But still they insisted on complaining.

They were in a vicious cycle. They complained because they weren't contented. And when God punished them for this attitude, they then complained all the more. God then had to punish them for their increased complaining. And so on it went.

No wonder life didn't get better! No wonder they spent forty years wandering through the desert! All that God required of them was obedience, praise, and worship; yet they failed.

The more I thought about it, the more uncomfortable I felt. Here I was, a Christian who was brought out of the bondage of sin by Jesus; I was fed, clothed, and taken care of; yet I hadn't been praising Him as I should. Maybe the second gentleman was right. Maybe things would get better if I would just begin praising God more consistently.

TWO

THE ONLY THING
WE HAVE TO FEAR

When I finally got settled down on Praise Avenue, I was delighted at what a peaceful neighborhood it was. Nobody seemed nervous about anything. Nobody was afraid. Nobody was uneasy.

"This is great!" I thought. "Many people just don't realize how completely free of fear they could be if they would just praise God instead of fretting and fearing."

I recalled how fear had almost destroyed my ministry before it even had a chance to get off the ground.

My greatest fear was the fear of people. Throughout my early life, I always had trouble talking to people. It was hard enough for me to talk with individuals, let alone a large audience. Nevertheless, God, in His mercy, delivered me from that which I feared most—people.

I can still remember the occasion. I was only eighteen at the time, but I had just experienced an unforgettable all-night visitation from God in my bedroom. About six-thirty in the morning, I heard my dad stirring in the kitchen downstairs, so I went down to tell him how the Lord spoke to me during the night, and called me to preach the Gospel.

Now my dad lived a rough life up to that time. The only time that I heard him mention God was when he cursed. He was a man of the world, a thorough-going sinner, who loved the bottle, gambling, infidelity, and other vices.

When I told him about God's calling me to preach, he walked over and looked me straight in the eye. Slowly, he inhaled his cigarette smoke, then turned his head and blew it across the room, still not saying a word.

Turning back to me, he said, "I don't see how you could ever be a preacher. You've always had trouble talking even to one person, and to be a preacher, you have to do a lot of talking."

I knew he meant that to discourage me. He was dead set against the idea of my becoming a preacher. There was never a Christian Gossett, not to mention a preacher—but I knew that God called me. Faced with my dad's opposition and scorn, I bolstered up enough courage to reply, "Dad, I know I can't talk well, but I do know that the Lord called me to preach, and by His help, that's what I'm going to do with my life: preach the Gospel of Jesus Christ." I hoped he would understand, but he didn't. I went back upstairs to my room, feeling very uneasy. There, alone, I turned to God's Word, and my eyes fell on this Scripture: *"Fear thou not; for I am with thee: be not dismayed; for I am thy God: I will strengthen thee; yea, I will help thee; yea, I will uphold thee with the right hand of my righteousness"* (Isaiah 41:10).

How this passage nourished my heart! If God was with me, I reasoned, I had no reason to fear.

This is one of the most exciting revelations that the Holy Spirit has ever given me—that fear can be defeated through praise. Fear is probably the most prevalent and destructive force in our society today. It is Satan's most common tool, making it Praise Avenue's number one public enemy.

I don't mean to suggest for a moment, though, that the fears of people are to be taken lightly. There are all kinds of fears. Just as cars come in a multitude of colors, makes, and models, so does fear come in an infinite variety of forms and magnitudes. No matter what the form though, fear can be successfully dispelled through praising God.

If fears aren't dealt with, they can become terrible monsters that rule your life and keep you in bondage. The imaginary things you fear can sometimes become real.

Fear failure, and quite likely, you will fail.

Fear old age, and chances are that your old age will be a miserable experience.

Fear heart failure, and more often than not, your heart will give out prematurely.

Fear is no joke. It is a fact often discussed in the Bible. Job, when he lost his family and all of his possessions, made a very revealing comment. He said, *"The thing which I greatly feared is come upon me, and that which I was afraid of is come unto me"* (Job 3:25).

Therein lies a little insight into Job's tragedies. Job, like so many of us, had fears. When Job let his fears grow, Satan was permitted to enter his life and translate those fears into reality. Unfortunately, Job didn't recognize this mistake until his fears came to pass.

Dr. Alexis Carroll, one of America's leading physicians, once stated, "Fear is capable of starting a genuine disease." How I agree with Dr. Carroll!

I am convinced that many people have been stricken with diseases simply because they feared them. People sometimes fear arthritis until they have arthritis. Others may fear a nervous breakdown until they have one. At other times, certain diseases will come about as the result of fearing something totally unrelated to one's physical health. I suppose that stomach ulcers are the most obvious example of this type of illness.

Fear, as I said, can take many forms. I have a friend, now a psychiatrist in Washington, D.C., whom I first met in the West Indies. Some time back, we got into a discussion about fear, and he related to me some unusual kinds of fear that his clients suffered from. For instance, he actually knew a man who suffered so greatly from a fear of dirt that he wouldn't shake hands with anyone, for fear they would contaminate him. He spent much of his time washing his hands, fifty to a hundred times a day. Eventually, he came to the point where he would hardly let members of his own family touch him!

How unfortunate that this man didn't know of God's tremendous victory over fear! It always hurts me when I think of the needless misery that this man and his family faced—just because he submitted to fear.

Unfortunately, many of God's children have opened themselves to the work of Satan through fear. My wife and I know an outstanding couple in the Lord's work who are bound by a spirit of fear. They have a condition called *toxicophobia*, the fear of being poisoned. Often they will not touch their food in fear that it has been poisoned. I've often thought about how much more effective their ministry could be if only they wouldn't have submitted to this fear.

Jesus told us that no man could serve two masters; he would hate one and love the other. I am convinced that you cannot effectively serve Jesus and be a slave to fear at the same time. However, if you're already in bondage to some fear, Jesus can deliver you.

The classic biblical example of this sort of deliverance is found in 2 Chronicles 20. King Jehoshaphat, who led the people of Israel to a victory in battle, was delivered from fear through the power of praise. Jehoshaphat was surrounded by three hostile armies. The people of Israel were greatly outnumbered, and things looked pretty bleak. But what did Jehoshaphat do?

First of all, he decided to ask the Lord what He thought should be done. The answer to Jehoshaphat's prayer came through a prophet named Jahaziel. The first words of the prophecy were, *"Be not afraid nor dismayed..."* (verse 15).

God knew that the greatest enemy of the people of Israel was neither the Moabites, nor the Ammonites, nor the inhabitants of Seir who were marching against Israel; rather, their greatest enemy was fear.

The Lord told His people that the battle was His, not theirs. In fact, the Lord told them, *"Ye shall not need to fight in this battle: set yourselves, stand ye still, and see the salvation of the LORD..."* (verse 17).

How great God is! He didn't tell them that He would help them to win the battle. He didn't tell them they were to do fifty percent of the fighting, and He would do the rest; no, He told them that He would fight the entire battle for them.

How did the people react? The Bible goes on to tell us, *"And the Levites...stood up to praise the LORD God of Israel with a loud voice on high"* (verse 19). King Jehoshaphat then *"appointed singers unto the LORD, and that should praise the beauty of holiness, as they went out before the army, and to say, Praise the LORD; for his mercy endureth for ever"* (verse 21).

Were the people scared? Of course they were. They were surrounded by three hostile armies which were bent on their total destruction. Nevertheless, the people of Israel praised the Lord anyway.

Notice also that they put their full trust in the Word of the Lord. The people who were sent out to praise the Lord weren't stationed behind the army where they would be safe. No, they were stationed before the army, relying on their praises to be a suitable habitation for an all-powerful God who would fight the battle for them.

And the Lord did win the battle for them. The armies of Ammon and Moab were confused, and began fighting with the inhabitants of Seir, until they completely destroyed one another.

When the battle was over, it took Jehoshaphat's people three days to collect all of the plunder.

The last act in the account is perhaps the most important. The people, after they finished collecting the spoils of the war, took an entire day off to bless and praise the Lord for all that He did for them.

When God delivers us from something we fear, we should always give Him the glory and praise for what He does. That's the way to live happily on Praise Avenue.

THREE

HOW TO GET A HOME ON THE AVENUE

An ancient story is told of a palace which had a marvelous pipe organ in it. The organ performed flawlessly for many years; but one sad day, it broke down.

Immediately, expert repairmen from all over the world were called to fix it. But though they all tried their best, none of them were able to successfully repair the organ. So there it sat in cold silence.

But then one day a man who looked like a beggar came to the door and inquired if he might have a chance to repair the organ. Because he looked like a vagabond, he was at first refused. Finally, though, the man of the house decided to let him try. "After all," he reasoned, "this man can do no worse than the others."

The stranger began to work on the organ. After a few hours, the inhabitants of the palace once again heard glorious music flooding the whole house. Everyone, from the lowest servant to the owner, came running to the console.

"Who are you," they asked, "that you could fix the organ when even the best specialists in the world could not do it?"

"I," replied the stranger, "am the man who built it."

Now let's stop for a moment. Before continuing this investigation of praise, it is very important that you are acquainted with the Lord of the avenue—the One who "built" it. His name is Jesus Christ. He's the One who makes the life of praise possible. We're not simply preaching a doctrine of mental optimism in this book. We're trying to introduce you to a person who can completely transform your life. Once you contact Him and know Him, you'll have good reason to offer praises to God.

You see, Jesus Christ not only made the life of praise possible, but He made you and me. Whatever needs to be "repaired" in us is simple work for Him. After all, He is the divine Son of God and the mighty second person of the Godhead. He gave His life to pay the penalty for all of our sins. But death could not destroy Him. The grave could not hold Him. He rose from the dead and was seen by many people. He then ascended into heaven, and will soon come again in power and glory to be united with all of His blood-bought believers, and we shall reign with Him forever.

Right now, I'm going to ask you an important question—probably the most important of your life. Who do you say Jesus is? Is He your personal Lord and Savior?

I trust that most of you can reply, "Yes, Jesus is my Savior!" If, however, you can't really answer that Jesus is your Savior—if you have some doubt in your mind—then let me assure you on the authority of God's eternal Word that you can be saved today! You can receive forgiveness for all of your sins, and start a whole new life this very instant!

"How?" you say.

First, I'm going to ask you to cast aside all of your private ideas and theories about how a person gets to heaven, and let me point out what the Word of God says.

The first truth is "strong medicine." But, friend, there is no way God can help us unless we are willing to believe what He says about us: that we are lost sinners on our way to eternal destruction. God tells us in His Word, *"...There is none righteous, no, not one,"* and again, *"...all have sinned, and come short of the glory of God"* (Romans 3:10, 23).

My message to you right now is the same one that Paul preached in Acts 20:21: *"...repentance toward God, and faith toward our Lord Jesus Christ."* All of the steps to salvation are summed up in those two simple words: repentance and faith.

When you turn from sin and turn to Jesus, He will come into you, forgive you, save you, cleanse you, make you anew, and fill your heart with praise. All you need to do is put your trust in Him.

But perhaps that's hard for you to do. Perhaps you're not sure if Jesus is really there for you. Or maybe you're not quite ready to stake all your hopes of salvation on Him.

I am reminded of a story that I heard about a weary traveler who was journeying in the early days of this country. This traveler came to the banks of the Mississippi on a cold winter's evening. The surface of the river was covered with ice, and he wondered whether the ice would bear his weight.

Night was falling, and it was urgent that he reach the other side. Finally, after much hesitation and with many fears, he began to creep cautiously across the surface of the ice on his hands and knees. He thought that he might thus distribute his weight as much as possible and keep the ice from breaking beneath him.

When he was about halfway over, he heard the sound of singing behind him. Out of the dusk came a man, driving a four-horse load of coal across the ice, singing merrily as he went on his carefree way!

Here was the first man—on his knees, trembling lest the ice not be able to bear him up; and there, as if whisked away by the winter's wind, went the man with his horses and coal, upheld by the same ice on which the man was creeping. The difference was that the man with the horse had tested the ice, and knew that it was well able to carry him and his load safely.

Friend, I have tested Christ. In every circumstance of life—in joy and sorrow, in success and failure, in health and sickness, indeed, in every conceivable type of situation—I have trusted Jesus, and have found that He was able to bring me and my burden safely to the other side. With Paul, I can say, "...*I know whom I have believed, and am persuaded that he is able to keep that which I have committed unto him against that day*" (2 Timothy 1:12). In other words, I know the ice won't break.

But you say, "I'm not really ready for Jesus. I don't think that I'm worthy to be His follower." Oh, how sorry I feel if that is what you are saying!

An imaginary story is told of a man who approached heaven's gates, and saw there a sign over the arch which said, "Admission, 1,000 points."

"Oh," he thought, "this is going to be easy," as he prepared to talk to the angel who was standing there.

The angel took down all the important statistics and said, "And now, tell me, what kind of person have you been?"

"Well," the fellow said, "I went to church almost every Sunday of my life. The only times I missed were when I was sick, and I have quite a string of medals here inside my coat to prove that I had a perfect record of attendance for forty years."

"Do you mean," said the angel, "that you never missed church once in forty years?"

"That's right," said the man.

"Wonderful!" replied the angel. "That will be one point."

"One point?" the man thought. "Only one?"

"Now," continued the angel, "tell me more." "Well," the man said, "I just figured up the other day that I gave over $50,000 to the church during my life time."

"You did that?" said the angel. "Wonderful, that will be two points. What else did you do?"

"Well," said the man, feeling very downhearted by this time, "I was a deacon in our church for thirty-five years, and during those years, I think I visited around 4,000 people in the hospital."

"You visited that many people?" the angel said. "That will be three points."

"Well," said the man in absolute discouragement," it looks like the only way a person can get in here is by the grace of God."

"That's it exactly!" said the angel. "One thousand points— enter thou into the joy of thy Lord!"

Now, obviously, this story has some theological faults. We don't mean to suggest that anyone can be saved at heaven's gates. This is an urgent matter that you need to take care of now. After death, it will be too late. But the truth of the grace of God is so important! There is no other way to be saved than through grace. We can never hope to make ourselves worthy of His love. But when we come to Him in repentance and faith, He will be merciful and save us immediately. No one is worthy of Jesus' love. No, not one. But don't give up. He still wants us, just the same. Read what Jesus said about this subject in Matthew's gospel:

And as Jesus passed forth from thence, he saw a man, named Matthew, sitting at the receipt of custom: and he saith unto him, Follow me. And he arose, and followed him. And it came to pass, as Jesus sat at meat in the house, behold, many publicans and sinners came and sat down with him and his disciples. And when the Pharisees saw it, they said unto his

disciples, Why eateth your Master with publicans and sin-
ners? But when Jesus heard that, he said unto them, They
that be whole need not a physician, but they that are sick.
But go ye and learn what that meaneth, I will have mercy,
and not sacrifice: for I am not come to call the righteous, but
sinners to repentance. (Matthew 9:9–13)

Friend, we are all *"publicans and sinners"* in the sight of
Almighty God. And there is no point in trying to justify ourselves
by good works. Why not simply accept the wonderful gift of salvation that Jesus is offering, and begin immediately to praise Him
for it?

Are you ready? All right, this is your moment. Bow your head
right where you are and tell Him all about it. Tell Him your sins;
tell Him your sorrows; give Him your burdens; ask Him to come
into your heart. He'll save you immediately.

Once you know the Lord, you'll certainly be eager to move
onto Praise Avenue. And He's got a place for you. You don't need
to wait until you get to heaven to start praising. You can begin the
life of praise right now.

FOUR

PERMANENT RESIDENCY

You can't *buy* property on Praise Avenue; you can only *rent* property. The *rent* is regular, heartfelt praise to God. And you can stay only so long as you keep praising.

And here's the rub: to keep on praising once you've begun! Most of us are good "starters," but not very good at sticking with it. We make splashy beginnings. But then in an off-guard moment, we begin to size up our circumstances and decide that they are somewhat less than ideal. Then comes the doubting, the grumbling, the grasping after something better, the traipsing all over town to find a "better lot in life."

Have you read the story of the house with golden windows? A small boy used to live in a cozy little house on a mountainside. Every morning he was fascinated by another house over on a yonder mountainside which seemed to have golden windows. And how he wished that someday he might live in a house with golden windows!

Well, one morning, he decided he would make that long walk over to the other mountain and find that house with those beautiful windows. So he walked and walked all day. Finally, he came to that little house. But what do you think? The windows weren't golden at all! They were just plain old glass.

The poor little fellow couldn't understand it. He thought that surely he must be at the wrong house. So he knocked on the door, and a little girl answered.

"'Tell me," said the little boy, "where's the house with the golden windows?"

Immediately, the little girl pointed back across the valley to the little boy's own house, and said, "There it is, way over there." The little boy looked, and sure enough, the setting sun was reflecting in the windows of his own house, and they looked like pure gold!

How often we get our eyes on some "house with golden windows"—some blessing we'd like to have—not realizing that if we'd just praise God and keep happy in Jesus, he would bring to us all the blessings we need.

Now, admittedly, that takes faith. It takes faith to keep on praising God in every situation, but not necessarily an advanced faith. Simple, childlike faith will do. And such a faith is probably the most important single possession that any Christian can have.

Faith and praise go hand-in-hand. In fact, praise is nothing more than the outward expression of your inner faith. You believe that God is taking care of you. You trust Him more than life itself. And because of that, you praise Him. Doubt is what causes praise to dry up.

So trust God as a child trusts his father. Don't make it complicated. Don't "work up a sweat" trying to get more faith. Use what you have. Relax and praise God. Thank Him in every situation, no matter how it looks. Simple faith is all you need.

One of the most interesting examples of this kind of childlike faith is George Müller of Bristol, England. The many accounts of his trust in the Father's faithfulness are awe-inspiring.

One time Mr. Müller was sailing on a ship across the Atlantic for a speaking engagement in Montreal. Toward the end of the journey, a heavy fog settled in, and the Captain advised the passengers that there would be at least a twenty-four hour delay in their arrival.

George Müller made his way to the Captain's cabin, and informed him that he was never late for an appointment, and that he quite expected to arrive on schedule in Montreal.

The Captain listened quietly, and then tried to explain the fog situation to Mr. Müller. To all of this, Mr. Müller replied, "Captain, I believe my heavenly Father wants me to be on time for my preaching engagement in Montreal. I shall pray and ask the Father to remove this fog."

The Captain explained that he, too, was a Christian, and would like to join him in prayer.

George Müller prayed simply, and with perfect, childlike confidence, "Father, I am scheduled to be in Montreal to preach Your Gospel on Sunday. The Captain informs me that the fog will delay our arrival by at least twenty-four hours. I have never missed an appointment for your business, Lord, and I expect that You will make it possible for me to be on time for this one. I ask You in Jesus' name to lift the fog. Amen." The Captain then began to pray, but George Müller stopped him. "Captain," he said, "there's really no need for you to pray, because you really don't believe anyway. I do believe; I have prayed; so it is done."

With that, the two went out to the deck. When they got there, they found that the fog had amazingly lifted!

Such is the simple, childlike faith that God honors. Childlike faith is indispensable to the praise life. The more childlike your faith, the greater will be your success in the kingdom of God. The more childlike your faith, the more quickly you will receive the mighty infilling of the Holy Spirit. Most important though, the more childlike your faith, the more readily you will please the Lord by "giving thanks in everything." So keep on believing and keep on praising.

I remember a series of crusades I scheduled on the island of Martinique in the West Indies. One of the first meetings was in the town of Francois, with large and unusually noisy crowds. The children were disorderly, and constant loud noises marred the effectiveness of the crusade. At the time, I found it very hard to praise the Lord, but nevertheless, I acknowledged the fact that He was still in control of everything, and would somehow bring good out of that situation. Yet, I knew that it would be extremely difficult to continue across the island if all of our crusades were as disorderly as the one in Francois.

During one of my private prayer and praise sessions, the Lord led me to call together the various ministers and missionaries who were to participate in our next crusade in the Martinique town of Rivière-Pilote.

When they gathered with me, I briefly explained the problem and then led them in a short praise offering to the Lord. Then I read to them Matthew 18:19, where Jesus says, *"Again I say unto you, That if two of you shall agree on earth as touching anything that they shall ask., it shall be done for them of my Father which is in heaven."*

Together, we agreed that peace, order, and respect would reign in the crusade at Rivière-Pilote, and that confusion and undue noise would be dispelled. Then I did something which has now become a habit with me. I led them in praising God for the victory which He promised to us.

When I finally stood before the multitude in Rivière-Pilote to preach the Gospel through my interpreter, I found that the Father had indeed done what we asked! The people gave perfect attention to my message, and whatever we asked them to do, they did readily. They were very reverent and responsive to the Gospel I preached. Eagerly, the crowds pressed forward to receive the Savior and be born again. What happened? Simple faith was expressed in heartfelt praise—and heartfelt praise released the power of God in that situation. Our problem was solved.

Once when I was conducting a crusade in Klamath Falls, Oregon, a Mrs. Harry Belau was brought to one of our services by her pastor. She was suffering from a severe heart ailment, and very weak.

When I was informed of Mrs. Belau's poor condition, I prayed for her in Jesus' name. After the prayer, I felt prompted by the Holy Spirit to tell her to run up the aisle of that large church auditorium.

Later, after I talked with her, Mrs. Belau told me that she was trying to think of a million excuses for not running up that aisle at that moment. First of all, she knew that she wasn't supposed to exert herself in any way because of her heart. Second, she wore a pair of high heels to church, and didn't want to run in them. Third, she was just plain embarrassed at the thought of running up an aisle with all of those people staring at her.

Nonetheless, Mrs. Belau, with a heart full of simple faith and praise, turned and ran up the aisle, praising God.

When she got to the end of the aisle, she realized that she no longer had any chest pains. She seemed to be in perfect health. How she praised God as she ran back down the aisle to the platform!

Since that time, she has had a few examinations to check the status of her health, and in every case, there has been absolutely no trace of a heart condition!

Every born-again Christian needs to get into the believing and praising habit. Keep on believing. Keep on praising. Praise God again and again. No matter what problem you're facing. Praise and praise until you have the habit firmly established. By faith and praise, you will sometimes find yourself zipping over some problems before you're even aware of them!

If you find that you lack the kind of faith that brings miracles, then I suggest that you try the following steps:

First, read your Bible often. Set aside a time each day to read it. As you read from your Bible, ask the Lord to use it to increase your faith. Each time that you open it, confess, "I believe that what is written is true, because God said it is true."

Second, try to get into as much good Christian fellowship as possible. Ask the Lord to guide you into the kind of glowing praise-fellowship that thrives on childlike faith.

Third, begin to exercise your faith. Don't treat faith as something which is to be wrapped up in a little box and set on a shelf. Use it! That is what God intended you to do. You'll never know how much faith you have until you have tried it out! Don't wait for others to do your believing for you.

Last, and perhaps most important, begin to praise God in all things. Don't rely on your feelings. Just do it, and keep on doing it, because the Word of God says that you are to do it. Praise God! Do it again and again. That's the way to be a permanent resident on Praise Avenue.

FIVE

HE ALWAYS ANSWERS

Not too long ago, a man came up to me after a meeting, and said, "Don, you keep talking about all of the times that God responded to your praises; now honestly, do you mean to tell me that each one of your prayers has been answered just exactly the way you wanted it answered? Are you honestly telling me that I can praise God for anything and He'll give it to me?" the man prodded.

"Of course I didn't say that," I replied. "What I did say was that God always answers my prayers and praises."

I watched for a moment to see whether he understood what I was saying.

"What's the difference?" he finally asked.

"Well," I replied, "there are really four answers that God might give His children on Praise Avenue. Unfortunately, most people misinterpret some of those four answers as just plain deafness on God's part. Don't ever let anyone kid you. God isn't deaf!"

The man seemed to be gaining interest, since he paused for a moment and asked, "So what are the four answers?"

"Well," I replied, "the first answer is the one that most Christians have grown to expect. That is the quick and simple 'yes' that God sometimes gives. For instance, God always says 'yes' when we request salvation or forgiveness for our sins. There isn't any time lapse. We know immediately that God has answered our prayers, because He has 'delivered the answer to our front door,' so to speak."

"Well, yes, it's easy to see how God responds to our praises in cases like that," my friend said, "but what about the other times?"

"That's where the other three answers come in," I replied. "God doesn't always say 'yes.' Sometimes He says other things."

"Such as?"

"Such as 'no.' God can and sometimes does say 'no.'"

"Aha! That's what I mean," my friend broke in. "You see—God doesn't always listen to our prayers!"

"Oh, but He does," I replied. "You see, to be able to say 'no' to someone, you have to be listening in the first place."

"Okay, so God is listening to me; what kind of an answer is that? For all I care, He might as well not be listening," my friend replied honestly.

I knew just how that man felt. There is a certain element of frustration in having someone say 'no' to you, even though that person may have done it for your own good. Nevertheless, we should be most thankful, and willing to praise God when He says 'no,' because it is a sign of His love for us.

Continuing on with the conversation, I said, "All right, let me give you an illustration. Do you have any small children?"

"Why, yes," he replied. "I have a son, Michael, who's three, and a daughter, Christina, who's four. Why?"

"Okay," I said. "Suppose that either Michael or Christina came up to you and asked for a can of gasoline; would you give it to them?"

"Heavens, no!" the man replied.

"Why not?" I asked him.

"Mr. Gossett," the man replied, "you know perfectly well why I wouldn't give them that sort of thing. Why, they might kill themselves!"

"In other words, you wouldn't give them anything that was harmful because you're a loving father," I commented.

I could see the light dawning in the man's eyes.

"Do you mean to tell me that God sometimes says 'no' to my prayers because I really don't know the danger of some of the things that I'm asking for?" he said.

"Exactly," I replied. "Now, what if your son or daughter didn't accept your 'no' and continued to beg for the gasoline? Would you give it to them?"

"Of course not," my friend replied.

"And what would be your reason?" I queried.

"Why, I wouldn't be a loving father if I didn't keep dangerous things away from them. So I'd just keep on saying 'no,' no matter how loudly they screamed at me," he said.

There was a brief silence as I waited for all of this to sink into my friend's consciousness. Suddenly, the silence was broken.

"Don," he said, "are you saying that some of us as Christians are actually taking spiritual tantrums, instead of just accepting God's answer?"

"Well, I have to admit that I've never heard it put that way," I said, "but it is a rather good analogy."

The two of us went on talking about that for a while before my friend sat bolt upright as though he just remembered something important.

"Don, you mentioned that there were four answers that God could give us; yet, we've only covered two. What are the other two?"

"Well, let's get back to the gasoline," I said. "Suppose that your son were about fifteen years older; how would you then react to his request for some gasoline?"

"Well, assuming that he were responsible, I'd probably give it to him," he said.

"But what's the difference between the first request and the second one?" I asked.

"Age," he replied.

"In other words," I said, "time."

"Exactly."

"You see," I continued, "God sometimes answers us by saying 'wait.' And He has His reasons for saying that. First, He may know that we aren't mature enough either mentally or spiritually to have what we're asking for right away. Or, he may know that there is a better time for the prayer to be answered."

"That's rather depressing," my friend commented.

"It just seems that way," I said. "You have to remember that God knows what He's doing. I've run into several cases where God has delayed a healing for a few days in order to further the cause of His kingdom. Why, just the other day, a woman came to ask for a healing, and when she was prayed for the first time, nothing happened. The second time, however, her whole family was with her. She was instantaneously healed, and her family accepted salvation as a result of it. Now, what do you think would have happened if God went along with her timing, instead of acting in His own wisdom?"

"Well, she might have waited a long time to see her loved ones accept salvation," my friend said. "The tough part of this waiting business, though, is that we don't usually know why God's making us wait."

"I'm glad you brought that up," I said "That is why we are told in 1 Thessalonians 5:18 to give thanks in everything. You see, when we praise God for everything that happens, we are, in effect, acknowledging Him as the One with the better judgment. We trust Him as our loving Father to make the best decisions for us.

"However, when we fail to offer up praises to the Lord for His 'wait' answers, we are like little children who refuse to acknowledge their parents' superior judgment, and keep demanding things which the parents know are harmful to them."

My friend seemed to be intrigued with the fact that true praise is, in reality, perfect submission to the will of God.

"Don," he said, "you still haven't told me what the other answer is. It seems as though we've covered the entire range already."

"Well," I told him, "we've covered the most important points, I'll grant you. However, there is one other kind of answer that God likes to give us. And it's probably the easiest to praise Him for."

"Ah, you mean when God gives us something better than what we had originally asked for?" my friend asked.

"Exactly," I replied. "It's as though you went to your father and asked him for five dollars, and he decided to give you ten instead. You certainly wouldn't argue with him. In fact, you'd probably be overjoyed. This is the kind of thing that God, our loving Father, likes to do the most."

By the time he left, I was confident that my friend would be able to praise the Lord for every answer to all of his prayers. I just wish that all of the residents of Praise Avenue could have the same trust and confidence in the wisdom and power of our Father.

If there ever comes a time in your life when you feel that God isn't responding to your prayers, I suggest that you try to look upon God as He is—a loving Father who wants the very best for His children. Don't try to peg God down to a specific act, and don't try to tell Him how much time He has to do something. He knows all about that. All He wants us to do is to love Him and praise Him for what He is—a loving Father.

SIX

KNOW-HOW FOR BEGINNERS

Some time ago, a man (I'll call him George) came to see me. "Mr. Gossett," he said, "I've heard you speak on praise several times. I believe what you say, but I really just don't know how to praise the Lord. I've never praised the Lord, except by singing in church."

The question hit me like a ton of bricks. For years, I had been teaching about the power of praise; yet I neglected to teach people how to praise.

"Well," I said, "let's get started right now. Say after me: 'Praise the Lord!'"

I think George was a bit surprised by our elementary beginning; nonetheless, he responded with a rather timid, "Praise the Lord."

"That's fine," I encouraged him. "Let's try it again."

We repeated this verbal offering to the Lord for several minutes, until my friend seemed to grow a bit more comfortable with it.

"Okay," I told him, "let's lift up our hands and do the same thing."

A look of distress crossed George's face. "But that's like the Pentecostals!" he blurted out.

I tried to point out to George that raising the hands was a very biblical form of praise, and that the Pentecostals only praise God with upraised hand because the Bible says that men are to *"pray every where, lifting up holy hands, without wrath and doubting"* (1 Timothy 2:8).

For the moment, I think George was wishing I hadn't pointed out that verse; nevertheless, he responded by gingerly lifting his hands while we praised the Lord.

"Now, here's a praise Scripture that tells us to clap our hands," I said. "Psalm 47:1 says, *'Clap your hands, all ye people.'*"

George looked even more distressed. "Don," he said, "they'd never let me do this sort of thing in my church."

"Well, then, do it in your own private worship," I told him. "It may seem a bit awkward at first, but the Holy Spirit will ease things for you. It will get easier for you as time goes on."

I'm not at all sure that George was convinced, but at least he was willing; I told him to do this often when he was alone—especially if he wasn't permitted such liberty in his church.

I think he was almost afraid to hear my next suggestion; nevertheless, he hung on.

I continued, "Did you know that the Bible tells us to shout for joy? In fact, shouting is one of the more frequently mentioned forms of Bible praise. The other forms can get mechanical if we're not careful, but rarely is shouting merely a ritual!"

With that, I led George in shouting praises to the Lord.

"Now, that's not all," I told him after we stopped. "There are even more ways to praise the Lord."

"Like what?" he replied.

I'm sure that George felt just as I felt when I first started to investigate the forms of praise. Surely God must have a broad imagination if He could think of so many ways for us to praise Him.

"Well," I asked, "can you play a musical instrument?"

He grinned, knowing what was coming. "I'm a bit rusty," he replied, "but I've played the trumpet since high school."

"Tremendous! Did you know that Psalm 150 tells us to praise the Lord with trumpets, organs, harps, tambourines, and cymbals? In fact, one of my friends plays a tambourine for the Lord quite often. I'm sure that the Lord is pleased with all of the other musical instruments too."

George was, I think, rather intrigued by the fact that there was so much evidence of the Lord's interest and pleasure in music. It turned out that his interest in music was a bit deeper than he led on at first.

As we continued our conversation, I sensed that George's interest in praise-life was growing. "George, just how interested are you in really praising the Lord?" I finally asked.

"Well," George replied, "I was interested enough to come over here and talk with you, if that answers anything."

"George, have you ever heard of the baptism in the Holy Spirit?"

"The what?"

George's reply was typical. He was obviously unfamiliar with the term.

"You know," I continued, "the Lord says in John 1:33, '*Upon whom thou shalt see the Spirit descending, and remaining on him, the same is he which baptizeth with the Holy Ghost.*'" God was, of course, referring to Jesus. And then in the first and second chapter of Acts, we have the account of the disciples being baptized in the Spirit on the day of Pentecost."

"Not to interrupt you, Mr. Gossett," George broke in, "but what does this have to do with praise?"

"Well," I went on, "one of the major effects of the baptism in the Holy Spirit is that it helps us to praise the Lord more effectively."

George looked momentarily pained. "You don't mean tongues, do you?" he said.

"Well, that's part of it," I said, "but not all. Praying in tongues certainly enables us to expand our praise life, but Ephesians 5:18–20 seems to tell a lot more of the story. Look them up when you get home. Those verses imply that the Spirit-filled life gives us a joy that makes it almost impossible for us not to praise the Lord."

There was a long silence as George shifted uncomfortably in his seat. Finally, he cleared his throat and spoke. "Supposing that you wanted the baptism in the Holy Spirit, just how would you go about getting it?" he asked.

"Well," I said, "in many cases, the baptism is ministered through the laying on of hands. However, that isn't always necessary. Since Jesus is the baptizer, and since He isn't restricted by men, many people receive the baptism without anyone's so much as touching them. This is what happened with Cornelius's household in Acts 10. The important thing is that you receive the Spirit in simple faith."

Suddenly, George stood to his feet, thanked me for my time, and quietly excused himself. After I was alone again, I found myself wondering if I had offended him.

Later though, I ran into George on the street. Immediately, I saw that something about him was different. I knew, even before he had a chance to tell me, that he had received the baptism in the Holy Spirit. Oh, the joy and praise that bubbled out of him as he told me about his new experience in the Spirit!

I admired George. He was able to overcome the natural pride that most of us are saddled with when we become adults. I suppose this is what Jesus was referring to when he told us that we must become as little children in order to enter the kingdom of God.

Little children never seem to have any hang-ups when it comes to raising their hands, shouting, singing, or playing music for the Lord. They aren't concerned with the way they look or sound to others. It's only when children begin to grow up that they are hardened by pride.

Probably the most beautiful display of mass humility that I ever witnessed (which led to true praise) came just before Palm Sunday a few years ago while I was on the island of Barbados.

Before I left to go there, I had written a letter to Holmes Williams, pastor of the Evangel Temple there, suggesting we hold a "victory march" through the streets of the community. This march resulted in one of the most glorious manifestations of God's power and blessing that I have ever experienced.

When I arrived, I found the people prepared with banners bearing such slogans as, "I am blessed with Heaven's best," "I rejoice in Christ, my choice," plus many others.

We marched for several miles up and down the hills. Thousands of people came out of their homes and stores to watch this "spectacular" of hundreds of Christians marching, singing, and giving witness of the Savior's love and grace.

Holmes Williams, formerly a prominent banker with the Canadian Imperial Bank of Commerce, was leading the march, while I spent most of the time in his car with two loudspeakers, inviting the people to our crusade. I would ask them such questions as, "Are you happy?" "Do you have peace in your heart?" Then, I'd tell them that "Christ is the answer."

On our way back to the Evangel Temple, I started leading the people in joyous praises to the Lord Jesus Christ.

"Let every happy Christian say 'Alleluia!'" I would say.

In mighty unison they would all say, "Alleluia!"

"Praise the Lord!" I would shout.

"Praise the Lord!" everyone said in agreement.

Over and over again, we would chant, "Glory to God! Victory in Jesus!"

It was absolutely beautiful.

Halfway back to the Evangel Temple, Holmes came running back to the car. "Don," he said, "this is tremendous! Keep them praising the Lord!'

I did. As they marched, hundreds of people were shouting the praises of the Lord. At the head of the march, Holmes was exhorting the people who came out of their houses to see what was happening and to praise the Lord with us. "Praise the Lord!" he would tell them. An amazing number of people accepted his challenge and joined us in offering up praises to God.

As we continued this powerful offering of praise to Jesus, the glory of God was flooding our souls. The people who had already marched several tiring miles up and down the hills were suddenly revived. Instead of dragging, they were marching with their hands raised—many of them virtually skipping for joy.

The more we praised Him, the greater the presence of God was manifested. It was like a mighty downpour of sheer glory, saturating our souls—a downpour which cleared the air for a great crusade to follow.

The description of this scene may sound like a display of emotionalism to some; others may brand it fanaticism; but to the hundreds of us who participated, it was "heaven come down" to our souls.

Our triumphant march through one of the most thickly populated regions of Barbados reminded me of that first Palm Sunday, when the people "...*took branches of palm trees, and went forth to meet him* [Jesus], *and cried, Hosanna: Blessed is the King of Israel that cometh in the name of the Lord*" (John 12:13). I also remembered how "...*the whole multitude of the disciples began to rejoice and praise God with a loud voice for all the mighty works that they had seen*" (Luke 19:37).

I suppose that back there in Jerusalem, the Pharisees, proud folks that they were, weren't too pleased with that display of "fanaticism." In fact, we are told that they appealed to Jesus, asking that He stop them, saying, "Master, rebuke thy disciples."

Today, as then, we all too often encounter proud and even religious folks who object to praise. If they had their way, they would rebuke us for praising the wonderful Lord Jesus Christ.

Well, don't expect to find any proud neighbors on Praise Avenue! Proud people don't praise. True praise thrives in the fertile soil of humility. The Christian who realizes that he is saved solely by the grace and mercy of God desires to praise Jesus for the great salvation he possesses.

People who seek to justify themselves before God by going through the pomp and pageantry of some religious ceremony rather than by simply trusting Jesus are seldom able to overcome the pride which keeps them from praising the Lord.

I've always enjoyed Jesus' reaction to the rebuke of the Pharisees. He answered, "*I tell you that, if these should hold their peace, the stones would immediately cry out*" (Luke 19:40).

In effect, He was saying, "If pride stands in the way of your praising Me, then I'll go elsewhere for praise. The humble stones along the road will speak out gladly." Rejection by God is, to say the least, a very dangerous thing. I am convinced that one of the easiest ways to incur God's wrath is to refuse to praise Him. I am also convinced that most people who refuse to praise the Lord do so because of pride. James, inspired by the Holy Spirit, tells us that "God resisteth the proud, but giveth grace unto the humble" (James 4:6).

I like to define humility as complete dependence on God. When one has this spirit of dependence and trust in the goodness of God, he can't help but praise the Lord in everything and for everything!

But let me add a word of warning. Many people who successfully overcome the barrier of pride and begin praising the Lord seem to get the idea that they are doing God some sort of favor. Beware of that attitude! That is pride all over again, only in a different form.

Doing what is expected of you is not the same thing as doing someone a favor. A fireman might put out a fire in your home, and you would naturally be grateful. However, you would never say that the fireman put out the fire as a favor! It was his duty. It was what he was expected to do.

So it is with God's people. We are exhorted in the book of Hebrews, "By him therefore let us offer the sacrifice of praise to God continually, that is, the fruit of our lips giving thanks to his name" (Hebrews 13:15).

That is our duty to God. That is what God expects us to do. However, as in the case of the fireman, this doesn't mean that God isn't grateful for our love and praises.

All of this goes to point out that Praise Avenue is not, and never was meant to be, an exclusive neighborhood. Instead, God meant for all of us to live there. I sincerely hope that pride isn't keeping you from moving into the spot that God has for you.

SEVEN

LOGS FOR THE FIREPLACE

Have you ever watched a log in a fireplace burning down to a bed of ashes? At first, the flames are hot and devouring. As the log burns on, however, the flames become tamer, and finally they die out completely. In the end, there are only coals and ashes left.

All too many former residents of Praise Avenue have allowed the fires of praise to die out. At first, they entered into the praise-life with true joy. They really blazed with the glory of God. As time passed, though, they let the fires die down. The joyful praise that once burned in their hearts slowly turns into a small bed of gray ashes.

Now, what should a person do if he finds that his praise-fire is dying down? Well, why not try heaping a little fuel on the fire? To help with this spiritual energy crisis, I am including eleven "praise logs" which I have found to be especially helpful in keeping the praise-fire burning within my soul. Whenever you feel the fire getting low, try drawing upon this pile of spiritual cordwood. Then begin to enter into the praise life anew. You and the cold world will notice an immediate difference.

Log #1: When you build a fire, it is important to start with very small "logs" called kindling. This wood will give the fire an extra boost, and will help you burn other, larger logs. Why not try this little piece of spiritual kindling in the fireplace of your heart? Just take the following passage and feed it to your heart. How? By reading and believing it.

Here's the kindling: Jesus said, *"I am come that they might have life, and that they might have it more abundantly"* (John 10:10). All of us have trouble believing that at times. We're continually tempted to look at our circumstances: bills, dwindling bank-balances, and the soaring costs of everything. The more you think about these depressing circumstances, the more the fires of praise die away. Soon, you begin feeling spiritually cold. What can you do? Why, hurry and get the fire re-kindled! Start thinking about the abundant life you have in Jesus. There's no need to dwell on what you don't have. Dwell on what you do have. You can praise God because you have abundant life in Jesus. Didn't He say that He came to give you abundant life? Aren't you a twice-born person? Hasn't God freely given you eternal life? As you meditate on John 10:10, you'll be burning good kindling that will help you keep the fires of praise going.

Log #2: Here's a nice big log that will burn nicely in your praise-fireplace: *"For God so loved the world, that he gave his only begotten Son, that whosoever believeth in him should not perish, but have everlasting life"* (John 3:16).

This is an especially useful log if you're ever tempted to feel unloved and unwanted. You can "burn" this John 3:16 log by sitting down and thinking about how much God loves you. In fact, it might be a good idea to insert your name where "the world" is mentioned. Go ahead and say it aloud: "God so loved Jim—Mary—Joe—Alonzo." God—the Creator of the universe—loves me! He loves me! He cares about me! He wants me! I guarantee you'll soon get so excited about God's love that you'll feel like throwing open the shutters on your home and shouting to everybody on Praise Avenue, "What a miracle! God loves me!"

Log #3: One of the surest signs that your praise-fires are burning too low is the tendency to worry. Most of us are susceptible to this temptation when we start thinking about the future. And when you stop to think of it, there are many things out there on the distant horizon that could be worried about! Next month's rent, next year's false teeth, old age retirement, and the rising costs of funeral expenses! You can worry yourself into spiritual coldness if you don't learn to cast your burdens upon Jesus.

Here's a log that will help you in such times of temptation: *"Fear thou not; for I am with thee: be not dismayed; for I am thy God: I will strengthen thee; yea, I will help thee; yea, I will uphold thee with the right hand of my righteousness"* (Isaiah 41:10). Now if that verse doesn't stop your worrying and get you to praising, I don't know what will! Why, what is there to worry about if you are being upheld by God's right hand?

Log #4: One of the less enjoyable experiences of fire-building comes when someone accidently puts wet wood on the fire. In no time at all, there is a cloud of strangling smoke—if the fire stays alive at all. Christians on Praise Avenue can run into the same situation, if they're not careful. The wrong fuel on the praise-fire will only tend to quench it. How can you tell whether your fuel is really good? By being sure you're using scriptural logs.

The entire praise life should be based upon Jesus' promise that the *"scripture cannot be broken"* (John 10:35). Have you ever praised God for the Scriptures? Aren't you glad that God hasn't left us to muddle through life as best we can without giving us a guidebook? When we need guidance, too many of us are running around asking our neighbors what to do instead of going to God's Word. Take your Bible and hold it to your bosom and say, "Thank You, Jesus, for this precious book! Thank You! The Scriptures will never be broken. Thank You, Father."

Log #5: If you're ever tempted to find fault with other Christians, you'll need to add this log to your fireplace quickly: *"...ye are all one in Christ Jesus"* (Galatians 3:28). Meditate on that. Let it burn. The same Holy Spirit who abides in you also abides in your fellow Christian. We are a single, living organism—energized, led, and moved by the same Holy Spirit. We belong to one another, and we need one another. Admittedly, we have faults and imperfections. Some of us are rather difficult to love. But those who deserve our love least are the ones who need it most. So begin praising the Lord for your brothers and sisters on the Avenue, and forgive their faults as God forgives you. Love makes the praise-fires burn more brightly.

Log #6: Almost every day, as you look out beyond the Avenue, you realize that the world is in a state of constant turmoil. Bad news comes at us from every direction. On the eleven o'clock news, you learn that a hundred employees were laid off at a local factory today. On the radio, you hear that Mrs. Jones was raped at the mall last night. In the newspaper you read that some teenagers over on the next block were caught growing marijuana on a back lot. Now that's enough to make anybody's praise-fires start sputtering. But here's a log that will burn well when such depressing news come your way: *"...the peace of God, which passeth all understanding, shall keep your hearts and minds through Christ Jesus"* (Philippians 4:7). Immerse your spirit in that verse. Dwell on it. Claim it. No matter what's going on "out there," the peace of God is keeping your heart and mind. Doesn't that make the fire burn better?

Log #7: *"I am the LORD that healeth thee"* (Exodus 15:26). Isn't that a good log? In this world of headaches and heart failures, how important it is that we keep on praising our way through this invasion of sickness and ailments! Nowhere in the world are people as healthy as on Praise Avenue; for when people praise Him, God unleashes healing and health.

But what if you get walloped with the flu? Well, don't let yourself fall into depression or despair. God is still on the throne! Our heavenly Father is *"the LORD that healeth thee."* Just repeat that verse again and again and let it sink into your consciousness. Praise God in your affliction. Praise unleashes the healing power of God.

Log #8: *"As thy days, so shall thy strength be"* (Deuteronomy 33:25). Here's a log that will be good fuel when you feel like you're having "one of those days." How often do we get up in the morning to discover that the car won't start, or the baby is sick, or the cat ate your goldfish? At such times, we often catch ourselves saying, "Oh, it's going to be one of those days!" And sure enough, it usually is.

I want you to know that you don't need to be depressed because of unfavorable circumstances. As we praise Him, God measures out strength for you based on the kind of day you're called upon to face. When you're having great trials, God wants to send great supplies of strength. So praise the Lord. No matter what sort of day it is today, the Lord promises abundance of strength. All we need to do is believe His word and praise Him for it.

Log #9: You ought to praise God often for the miracle of life. Psalm 150:6 commands: *"Let everything that hath breath praise the Lord."* Praise Him for your breath, first of all. You're alive! Your lungs are faithfully pumping air into your system every day without a bit of attention from you. Take a big, deep breath of air right now and praise Him for two good lungs!

It might also be a good exercise in awareness to place your hand over your heart. For a few moments, just close your eyes and listen to the rhythmic thump-thump of that marvelous muscle that tirelessly pumps blood throughout your body, hour after hour, day after day, year after year. Life is a very precious possession. It's God gift to us, and we ought to praise Him for it. Don't ever take life for granted.

Log #10: *"God is our refuge and strength, a very pleasant help in trouble"* (Psalm 46:1). Now there's a log that will warm your soul on the coldest and bleakest of days!

Suppose, for instance, that you're driving home from work some rainy evening, when you lose control of your brand new car and skid into the car in front of you. Or suppose a telegram arrives some night, informing you that mother has passed away. Or suppose your teenage daughter, whom you've raised to be a good Christian, breaks your heart by marrying an unbeliever.

Most of us face crises of one kind or another as we go through life. But these crises need not overcome us if we will just remember that God is a very present help in trouble. He's not far away, even though it might seem so. He's very present. He loves to manifest Himself in times of trouble. So dare to praise God for that promise, even in times of tragedy. God can change the darkest night into golden dawn if we'll just praise Him.

Log #11: Suppose you owned a fireplace, and someone offered you a lifetime supply of cordwood—a little at a time, for as often as you needed it. Wouldn't you be grateful? I'm sure you would.

Now, God has done something far better than that for all the residents of Praise Avenue. Ephesians 1:3 tells us that *"God...hath blessed us with all spiritual blessings in heavenly places in Christ."* That sounds to me as though God has promised enough "logs" to keep our praise-fires burning from now until we get home to glory! Notice that God didn't say, "I've blessed you with half of the blessings," or "I've blessed you with most of the blessings." No, He said, "all spiritual blessings." Isn't that amazing? Isn't that something that makes you want to praise Him?

In this chapter, I have given you eleven praise logs. But every promise in the Word of God is a good log that will "burn" well, if you meditate on it and enjoy the glow of its warmth. So if you're beginning to feel cold, just go to the Bible and find another log. There's plenty of wood there to keep us all warm in the Spirit.

EIGHT

WHAT'S IN A NAME?

I'll never forget the time our neighborhood was being plagued by a vicious prowler. In spite of an intensive police follow-up, night after night the prowler would break into the home of some unsuspecting woman. His forays would often end in the tragedy of rape and injury.

Traveling all of these years as an evangelist, I have often been forced to leave my wife. So it was that my wife found herself alone one night while this man was on the loose.

That particular night, my wife had family prayer with our five children and put them to bed. She was just about to go around locking all the doors when she suddenly heard a man entering the house.

She froze. She told me she would have screamed had she been able, but she was so terrified that she couldn't make a sound. We didn't have any near neighbors anyway.

As she stood there, paralyzed with fear, suddenly the Holy Spirit came upon her and she heard herself say in a strangely hollow tone, "In the name of Jesus Christ, I rebuke you. I command you to leave my house at once; go, and leave me alone!"

Suddenly, as if some unseen force grasped the man, he stopped, turned, and fled out the door.

Words cannot describe the joyful praise that my wife and I gave to the Lord for the power in His name when I returned home! For many years, we had been praising the name of the Lord as commanded in Psalm 148:13, but somehow, until that night, we never realized the awesome power and authority of the name of Jesus.

I used to wonder how it was that a mere name could be powerful. In our world today, I thought, people are powerful, machines are powerful, and explosives are powerful; but how are names powerful? As I was meditating on this one night, the Lord gave the answer to me.

Just imagine that you are driving down the street, and you accidently go through a stop sign or a red light. You haven't proceeded more than half a block when you hear a siren blowing behind you; a quick glance into your rear view mirror reveals a policeman preparing to pull you over. Almost automatically, you pull to the curb and stop.

Now that policeman is a man just like you. Why, then, should we have to stop when he blows his siren? (Aside from the fact that he may be carrying a gun!) Well, the reason is quite obvious. That man represents an authority which is far greater than himself. Without his badge and uniform, he would have no authority at all to make you stop. However, when he wears the badge and uniform, he carries the awesome power of a higher authority—an authority that has the power to enforce laws and exact penalties for disobedience.

My friend, do you realize that Almighty God has given His children a badge and uniform of authority? Do you realize that you represent the highest power in the universe? Do you realize that all things are subject to you in the wonderful name of Jesus? What did Jesus say? *"Verily I say unto you, Whatsoever ye shall bind on earth shall be bound in heaven: and whatsoever ye shall loose on earth shall be loosed in heaven"* (Matthew 18:18). Doesn't that make you want to praise Him, to know that God allows you to act in His behalf? Aren't you grateful that God has given you such authority?

I've always enjoyed the reaction of the seventy disciples when they found out that they had this authority. Luke 10:17 tells us, *"And the seventy returned again with joy, saying, Lord, even the devils are subject unto us through thy name."*

I take considerable comfort in the fact that the disciples were overjoyed about the power of the name of Jesus after they actually saw what it could do.

If you're a Christian and don't see clearly why you should be praising the name of Jesus, perhaps this is an indication that you haven't done much in the authority of His name.

Why not start right now to rejoice and thank God for the fact that He is willing to entrust His name with you? Do you realize the responsibility that such an honor holds? Dear friend, it is not only a privilege to use the name of Jesus, it is a duty. For a Christian to neglect using the name of Jesus to heal and deliver is the same as a neighborhood policeman sleeping while on duty!

Now if God has given you His power, don't you think He will hold you responsible for neglecting to minister to others in the powerful name of Jesus? You need to go out as often as possible and minister in His name.

One evening in a meeting, a fellow told me he couldn't see the exact reason for praying all of our prayers in the name of Jesus. "Isn't that a rather mechanical thing to do?" he asked.

Oh, how my heart ached for that fellow! Friend, it is actually a privilege to pray in Jesus name! It should never be a mechanical drag.

One of the best reasons that I ever heard for praying in the name of Jesus came in the form of a delightful analogy. Suppose you are the king of a great country, and you must sort through your own mail every day. Most of the letters are in regular business envelopes, although a few are in personal envelopes of assorted sizes and colors. One day, as you are thumbing through your mail, you notice an envelope which you immediately recognize as your own royal stationery! You know that such stationery is used only by those with proper authorization. So you give that letter immediate attention.

Now, friend, we are sons of the King, and we have been authorized to ask in the name of Jesus. Jesus said, *"If ye shall ask any thing in my name, I will do it"* (John 14:14). That's the royal stationery! This isn't some sort of burdensome duty. This is a privilege! This is something for which we ought to praise God!

People all over the world are striving to make friends in high places; yet do you realize that, as one of God's children, you have a Friend in the highest office of all of creation? Do you realize that your Friend loves you, and only desires your love and praises in return? Do you realize that, as children of God, we have the right to unlimited protection and blessings?

I first came to realize the authority of the name of Jesus through a prayer request that came to me many years ago. I was called upon to pray for a boy who had been given up to die of brain tumors by the specialists at Barnes Hospital in St. Louis, Missouri. This boy was brought by his parents to Joplin, Missouri, where I was ministering at the time. In the name of Jesus, I cursed those tumors. There was no immediate, apparent change in the boy at the time. However, when his parents took him back to the hospital, they were told to their amazement and delight that the tumors disappeared. There wasn't even a trace of them!

F. B. Meyer used to tell this story: "Standing before a vast audience, the great Paganini broke string after string on his violin until only one was left. Holding up his instrument, he said, 'One string and Paganini.' Then he played magnificently as if it was fully strung." So today, we are often amazed at what can be accomplished by one Christian in the name of Jesus.

A woman was brought to me who was dying of cancer. She was in the last stages of the disease. Her skin was all discolored and seemed to be stretched over her bones. She had almost given up all hope of ever being healed.

I turned to John 14:13, where Jesus said, *"And whatsoever ye shall ask in my name, that will I do, that the Father may be glorified in the Son."*

I said, "Dear sister, Jesus said, *'You ask in my name, and I will do whatsoever you ask.'* Let's make the 'whatsoever' be for those cancers that are destroying your body and life. Jesus said, 'You do the asking, I will do the doing.' He is big enough to do anything we ask Him to do."

The woman gave me a quiet smile of assurance and said weakly, "That sounds good to me."

Together, we asked God to remove the cancer in Jesus' name. Within three days, it happened. The cancer passed from that woman's body! Today, she is a healthy, normal person who delights in praising God for the power in His name.

When I see such miracles worked by the name of Jesus, I wonder how anyone could possibly neglect praising the Lord. In fact, I'm amazed that it should even be necessary for God to command us to praise His name!

Oh, how I pray that all my brothers and sisters in Christ will not only begin to realize the power that is given to us, but will also begin giving God the rightful praise for the authority of His holy name!

NINE

PRAISE EVERY DAY KEEPS THE DOCTOR AWAY!

One of the most startling examples of the power of praise which I have run into is the case of Harry Erickson of Gold Beach, Oregon.

Harry spent seventeen years as a logger in the lumber camps of the Pacific Northwest. He found himself pinned under a load of logs which had fallen from a logging truck. Miraculously, though, he jumped aside quickly enough to escape the full blow.

However, even after surgery, Harry's leg was crooked and deformed, with the foot permanently extended to one side. The right leg was two and a half inches shorter than the left.

Sometime later, the Erickson family was invited to attend services at the Gold Beach Assembly of God and accepted Jesus as their Savior.

Then one night, Harry was prayed for during a revival I conducted at his church in Gold Beach.

After prayer, we asked him, "What can you do now that you couldn't do before?"

Harry replied, "Mr. Gossett, if I can get up on my right toes, then that's something that I couldn't do before."

Harry tried it.

Upon finding that he could do so, he was immediately beside himself with joy, praise, and gratitude to God. Then, as he turned to go back to his seat, I noticed that he decided to leave the auditorium and go into the adjoining prayer room.

Several minutes later, he came back into the auditorium—running! He was so overjoyed that I asked him what happened in the prayer room.

"Well," he replied, "I fell on my knees and dedicated my whole life to this wonderful Lord who could do such a great miracle. As I knelt there, our Sunday school superintendent came into the room and said, 'Harry, get up and let's see what God has done.' Well, I got up, rolled up my pant leg, took off my shoe and sock, and looked at my leg. And do you know what?"

"What?" I said.

"Every bone was straight and normal! The twisted foot was straight, the swelling was gone, and my leg was the same length as the other one!"

Harry, weeping for joy, demonstrated to the audience what Christ had done for him. The people were electrified, since many of them were aware of his former crippled condition.

The next morning, while walking on the beach, Harry started to watch his footprints in the sand. Ever since the accident, his right footprint had been crooked, but now it was different.

As he told me, "When I looked and saw two straight, normal footprints behind me, I couldn't keep from shouting the praises of God."

Harry's case, though startling, was by no means unique.

While I was engaged in a large tent meeting in California, I met a minister named Jack Neville, whose testimony was a real blessing to me. Jack was involved in a serious train wreck in Fresno.

Along with the other accident victims, Jack was rushed to the hospital. The doctors took X-rays and discovered that he was in a critical condition. When they realized he was a minister, they felt that they could level with him about the severity of his condition.

"Reverend," they said, "we want you to know what the X-rays revealed. Your back is badly broken. In your present condition, we're not certain that you'll make it. If you do live, you'll probably never walk again."

My minister friend had been well-experienced in coping with the unexpected, but this was simply too much!

He felt inwardly crushed.

As he rehearsed those words over and over in his mind, he found himself crying, "Oh, God, the doctors told me that I may not live. And, Lord, they said that even if I do live, I'll probably never walk again. Lord, I'd rather You take me home today. My life is Yours to preach the Gospel. But with the knowledge, Lord, that I won't be able to stand in the pulpit any longer, I'd prefer to die today."

As he continued pleading with God to take his life, the words from Matthew 8:17 flashed in his mind: "...*Himself took our infirmities, and bare our sicknesses.*"

As he meditated on this truth, the reality of it broke through to his heart. The Holy Spirit revealed to him that Jesus had actually taken his injuries upon Himself when He died on the cross. Jesus Himself took our infirmities and bore our sicknesses, our diseases, and our afflictions.

As the wonder of this great truth gripped his heart, fresh hope sprang up. Suddenly, he was transformed from a self-pitying Christian into a rejoicing believer who discovered what a great Redeemer he had, and what a mighty redemption the Lord provided!

The significance of the bleeding wounds of Jesus held his attention. The truth, "*with his stripes we are healed*" (Isaiah 53:5), was no longer a worn-out phrase to him. Each word throbbed with life and healing for his broken body! He began praising the Lord with his whole heart.

In each praise-session, he would say, "Dear Jesus, if You took my infirmities and carried my sickness in Your own body, then I don't need to bear them. Lord, it just isn't necessary that I endure this broken and crushed body, when You have already taken this suffering upon Yourself. Oh, thank You, Jesus!"

After some time, he made a decision: there was no need for him to remain in that hospital with that hopeless verdict upon his life. According to the promises of God, he had already been healed. Why should he remain captive to that bed?

Finally, he exercised his faith and began feeling a transformation! With praises to Jesus flowing from his heart and mouth, he stepped down on the floor and found that he was amazingly strong!

Quickly, he dressed, and walked out of the hospital room. In the hall, he met his attending nurse. She looked at him as if she had seen a ghost. "Reverend Neville," she protested, "you—you can't!"

"Can't what, nurse?" he replied.

She didn't appear to hear him. "Your legs, your back, Reverend—they're broken! It's impossible! Oh, dear! Get back to your room before you fall over dead!"

"Thank you, nurse," he replied, "but I'm walking out of this place. You see, Jesus, my Great Physician, paid me a visit and made me whole."

With those parting words, he proceeded down the hallway to the checkout desk. Before he could complete his checkout, however, the nurse summoned his attending physicians. They rushed over to the desk, approached him with caution, then appealed to him. "Reverend, we don't know what happened, or how you walked down here, but we do know your condition—you just can't do this."

They already called for a stretcher. When it arrived, they tried rather desperately to get him to lie down on it. Once again, though, he shared his testimony: "Jesus, the Great Physician, paid me a visit and made me whole." Seeing him standing there straight and whole, then bending over to demonstrate how strong he was, they couldn't deny it.

Later, he returned to the hospital for X-rays and an examination. The doctors could find nothing wrong with him. They agreed: "mysteriously," the Great Physician had done a work in him.

Not all of the healings that I have discussed on Praise Avenue have been as spectacular as Jack's or Harry's. Only recently, I was talking with a gentleman named George Billowus. George told me of how the Lord healed his arthritis. I think that you'll agree with me that this is a miracle of God, although it happened more quietly.

"Four years ago," George told me, "the doctors gave me up."

"What was wrong?" I asked.

"Arthritis. It had me down so bad that I was on crutches. I suffered great pain all over my body. Don, I was miserable."

When I asked him how he was healed, his face brightened as he replied, "I really believe that it was the faith and praises of my little granddaughter that brought me along. Cindy, who was three years old, and her two-year-old sister, Sandy, were at the house. I took little Cindy to the bedroom with me to take an afternoon nap. But she wouldn't go to sleep. She wanted to climb all over me, and I had to protest because I was in so much pain that it hurt even when people touched me.

"After a few minutes, though, she got over on her own side of the bed—but she kept rolling around and shaking the bed. Finally, I said to her, 'Cindy, you'll have to lie still or else I'll have to ask you to get up from the bed, because you're causing me an awful lot of pain.'"

"'But, Grandpa,' she replied, 'I was just praying for you. Jesus will make you better, and then me and Sandy can jump all over you, and you won't hurt anymore.'"

George's eyes glistened with tears as he continued his story.

"I was both touched and amused by the knowledge that she was praying for me so that she and Sandy could have the unlimited privilege of jumping all over me! And, you know, I believe that childish testimony was sweet praise in the ears of God, for within two months I was completely healed. I could get down on the floor, and both Cindy and Sandy could climb over me and have the greatest time!"

The more I thought about what George and the others told me, the more I understood the role that praise played in their healing. Praise is really the language of thanksgiving.

If you need a healing, then the best way to receive it is in the same way that you would receive any other gift—with thanksgiving. The best way to express our thanks to God is through praise.

It's sad, but true, that although most everyone wants to be healed, not everyone remembers to give God the glory for the healing.

When Jesus touched the fevered body of Simon Peter's mother, *"she arose and ministered unto them"* (Matthew 8:15). I am convinced that one of the primary reasons why Jesus heals people today is so that they can minister to others for His glory. Sometimes, the only ministry to which a person is called is simply telling others of the healing they received and Who it was who did it: Jesus. In this way, God gets the praise, and Jesus is lifted up.

TEN

HE'S A LIAR AND A THIEF

A sunny young couple approached me after the first service of an evangelistic crusade. With them was their small son, looking just as happy as his parents.

"Remember us?" the young father asked. Then, without waiting for an answer, he went on to remind me how I prayed for his little boy the year before.

"Don," he said, "you have no idea how happy we've been since last year. Tommy (name changed) is back in school and is doing great. The change is so amazing, I can hardly believe he's the same person. I—I—just don't know how to express the way we feel!"

"Well," I told him, "why not start by praising the Lord?"

"Oh, we've been doing that, Don," the man said. "Believe me; we've really been getting into the praise life!"

"Well, I couldn't think of anything better to do," I said.

Exactly a year before, this wonderful young couple brought their nine-year-old son to one of our meetings. When they came to me in the prayer line, they told me a heartbreaking story.

Their little son had been absolutely uncontrollable. He had been expelled from school, and often had to be tied with a rope to keep him from destroying everything in sight. His parents took him to a psychiatrist who eventually gave up, saying nothing could be done for him.

As the parents explained this boy's case to me, I became aware, by the Spirit of God, that here was a little boy who was under demonic attack.

As I looked at the boy, I could see the burning fire in his eyes. It was unreal. He was like an animal that went mad. As I stood there with those grief-stricken parents and their sick son, I began doing something that must have sounded strange to them. I began to praise the Lord for His power.

As I did so, the boy grew increasingly restless. Realizing that harm might come to the boy if I didn't act quickly, I promptly issued a stern command: "In the name of Jesus, I charge you demons to come out of this boy. Satan, you have no right to control this boy any longer. In the name of Jesus Christ, I command your full power over this boy to be broken." Then, looking the boy in the eyes, I said, "In the mighty name of Jesus, be loosed, set free, liberated!"

The results were instantaneous, and quite dramatic. The boy immediately relaxed, and a sweet smile of peace spread across his little face. Then, he did something that he hadn't done for years. Turning to his parents, whom he had rebelled against more times than they could count, he hugged them! Jesus broke the bonds!

According to the Bible, one of the important signs we're to watch for in the end times is an overwhelming increase in demonic activity. This is something that we should be aware of (but not afraid of). Those that walk on Praise Avenue have an enemy. There is a personality who does not want you to be praising God. There is someone who stands to lose by your praises. That someone is Satan.

Even some modern scientists are beginning to recognize the factual existence of evil, supernatural powers in the world—a fact which the Bible speaks of again and again. The Bible affirms the existence of the personality of Satan, and describes his origin, characteristics, and activities. He is described as the Adversary, Oppressor, Deceiver, Thief, Accuser of the Brethren, Destroyer, Prince of the Power of the Air, Tempter, Defamer, and the Father of Lies.

Now, dear friend, I don't want you to shrink back in fear as you read this. That's what Satan would like you to do. Rather, I want you to begin praising God all the more because God's Word assures us that *"greater is he that is in you* [the Lord], *than he that is in the world* [Satan]" (1 John 4:4). Now isn't that an extremely good reason for you to praise God?

Now, while you're not to be afraid of your enemy, neither should you be ignorant of his strategies. You should know that the Devil is out to deceive you. He's very smooth about this. He continually tries to make you think that certain kinds of sin are really "not so bad." He tells you that some of your disobedience is merely trivial, something that you shouldn't be concerned about. He warns you about developing an "oversensitive conscience."

He's like a man I heard of who kept promising his niece that he would remember her generously in his will. After he died, however, she discovered that most of his fortune had been left to others in the family, while she was given only a meager sum. "Well," she said glumly, "I might have known—soft soap is usually half lye."

That comment pretty well sums up the deceitfulness of Satan. Don't accept his "soft soap." As Jesus said concerning him, *"...There is no truth in him...for he is a liar, and the father of it"* (John 8:44). Therefore, you ought to steadfastly refuse every proposition he makes to you. Believe only what God says in His Word. Saying no to the Devil while persistently praising God will surely bring the victory. *"Resist the devil, and he will flee from you"* (James 4:7).

We also need to remember that Satan is out to destroy us, our families, and every born-again Christian. Jesus said in John 10:10,

"The thief [Satan] *cometh not, but for to steal, and to kill, and to destroy."* He does this by marring the image of God in people; by twisting and tangling people's minds; by saturating lives with filth and rot; by dragging souls into a Christ-less eternity *"where there is weeping and wailing and gnashing of teeth"* (Matthew 13:42).

Satan uses human instruments to destroy the human family. It seems unbelievable that men would yield themselves to the Devil as instruments to destroy their on fellowmen. But they do. Some peddle drugs at high schools to thrill-seeking teenagers. Others sell booze over the counter to anyone who can "prove" he is of age. Still others unashamedly sell pornographic material to idle college students.

How often our boys and girls are corrupted and robbed of their purity of heart before they reach the high school age! Nothing is left pure and holy for them! That is why I urge you to know your enemy.

Recognize the powers of evil for what they are—evil spirits sent by Satan to destroy!

Now, let's recap. What are we, as Christians, supposed to do when we come up against these demon powers of Satan? What specific things can we do?

First, we must exercise the authority that is ours through the name of Jesus. Jesus told us in Mark 16:17 that *"these signs shall follow them that believe; in my name shall they cast out devils."* We are also told in Philippians 2:9–10 that *"God also hath highly exalted him* [Jesus], *and given him a name which is above every name: that at the name of Jesus every knee should bow, of things in heaven, and things in earth, and things under the earth."* Therefore, when Satan lies to us, attacks us, and tries to destroy us, we ought to rise up in the name of Jesus and command the "father of lies" to leave us.

Second, we must rely upon the Word of God. Jesus, when tempted in the wilderness, quoted the Scriptures as a means of fighting the temptations of Satan. I suggest that you too stand upon the

Word of God when battling Satan. The Word of God is truth, and Satan has no defense against it.

Third, we must enter into true praise. Obviously, though, your praise might not flow as easy as it usually does when you're under attack. Praising God is the last thing that Satan wants us to do. But do it anyhow! When you praise the Lord, remember that your praises are inhabited by God, and all demon powers must flee! Just think of it: Satan can't stay where there is praise! And that is a good reason to begin praising the Lord!

Fourth, make it your prayer, along with David, "*Renew a right spirit within me*" (Psalm 51:10). Often, several times a day, pray this Bible prayer, for it is quite easy to allow a wrong spirit to come into our hearts. A spirit of pride, self-justification, anger, bitterness, unkindness, jealousy, unforgiveness, fear, and many other wrong spirits may begin manifesting themselves in our lives. This is another reason why I urge Christians to enter into a full life of praise.

And one more thing: don't just limit your praise life to a certain period of the day (even though a definite period is a very good idea). Rather, try to praise God for each event in the day. When frustration strikes, praise God! When anger creeps up, praise God! When pain takes hold, praise God! Satan won't stay around very long when you keep praising the Lord.

ELEVEN

DEFEATING DEFEAT

Almost every street has a back fence gossip who makes it her business to spread bad news and gloomy rumors throughout a neighborhood. So it is with Praise Avenue.

Even the most determined one who prays will find himself "pulled down" by the complainers and critics who live on the bordering alley called "Grumbling Street." It isn't easy to live in constant praise. Complaining is a subtle sin. Sometimes you discover that you've fallen into complaining without being aware of it. How does this happen? For some of us, I suspect it goes something like this:

Across the alley, on Grumbling Street, is a woman named Sue. "Sad Sue," everyone calls her, because she never seems happy. Every day, Sue spends most of her time leaning over the fence in her backyard, complaining to the neighbors. It doesn't matter what is going on, or what sort of day it is, Sue usually has a complaint to fit every situation. Is it warm and sunny outside? Sue will tell you she just can't stand the heat. Is it cold and damp outside? Sue will complain that the sun hasn't shone for two weeks.

Now I suppose that this sort of conduct wouldn't be half as harmful if Sue would just keep her opinions to her own street. But this is not the case. Time and again, Sue leans over the back fence and brings ill tidings and gossip into the lives of her neighbors on Praise Avenue.

One day, Sue drapes one arm over the fence in your backyard and says, "Mary, this just ain't my day!"

"Oh, my," you say, "is something wrong?"

"No, everything is wrong," she replies. "Got up an hour late this morning; burnt the toast; argued with the old man at breakfast; and now the washing machine won't work!"

"Oh, you poor dear!" you exclaim. "May I do something to help? You're welcome to use my washing machine!"

"Won't do any good," Sue sighs glumly. "It just ain't my day." Then, looking over her spectacles, she adds, "And it ain't gonna be yours, either."

"But what makes you say that?" you ask in surprise.

Pausing for a moment to rub a wart on her chin, she asks solemnly, "Don't you know it's Friday the thirteenth?"

"It is?" you reply.

"Yep. Nothin' ever goes right on Friday the thirteenth. You wait. It'll getcha before the day is over."

"Oh, I don't think so," you reply. "You see, I'm just not superstitious."

"Don't make no difference," Sue replies. "When somethin' bad is due to happen, there ain't nothin' you can do to stop it. You just gotta take it."

After that encounter, you're more careful about talking with "Sad Sue." But one day, Sue starts talking about "religious things" and quite an interesting conversation develops.

"I hear you got a new preacher at your church," Sue begins.

"Oh, yes," you reply. "You just must come to hear him. You'd love his sermons."

"What time does he get done preaching?" Sue inquires.

"Usually around twelve-thirty, why?"

"Hmph! That'll be the day when I'll sit in church that long. Ain't he supposed to be done at noon?"

"Well, yes, I guess so, but sometimes he just gets so filled up with the blessings of God that he can't get stopped on time."

"That's the way with all them preachers. Doesn't that get on your nerves when you've got a roast in the oven and the kids are squirming all over the pew wantin' to know when they can go home?"

"Well—it does bother me a little sometimes," you reply hesitantly.

"Sure it does!" Sue smiles broadly. "Some of these preachers just don't exercise common sense when it comes to the length of their sermons. Sometimes they seem to forget that it's almost impossible to keep kids until after twelve o'clock."

"Yes, I'll admit that's true," you reply thoughtfully.

"You know," Sue says, shaking her finger at your nose, "if this world was gonna be saved by sermons, it would have been saved years ago. The trouble with most of the sermons nowadays is that there just ain't no power there. You know what I mean?"

"Yes, I'll have to agree with you there," you admit.

"That's why the whole world's going to pot the way it is," Sue concludes. "The churches just don't have no power anymore."

As the weeks pass, you find yourself beginning to take on some of "Sad Sue's" bad habits. You attend your prayer and praise meetings with a long face. Noticing that things seem cold and lacking in power, you immediately begin praying, "Oh, Lord, what's the matter here? Things seem to be so tied up. Lord, I feel such darkness here. It's as though this place were filled with evil spirits."

One day, your brother, Hal, stops by to discuss this with you. He points out that your prayers are becoming very, very negative.

"Mary," he says, "do you realize that when you complain to the Lord, you are actually giving glory to Satan?"

"Oh, but I didn't mean it that way," you say.

"I'm sure you didn't," Hal replies. "But that still doesn't do away with the fact that you're becoming so much like 'Sad Sue' that you're in danger of being evicted from Praise Avenue!"

Together, Mary and Hal pray for her forgiveness, and begin to praise the Lord. Mary wipes the tears from her eyes and says, "I'm sorry, Hal. I should have known better. I guess I didn't realize how sour my spirit was becoming. From now on, I'll try to be more careful about Sue. She just needs Jesus, that's all."

Friends, all of us who live on Praise Avenue must be constantly on the lookout for the gloomy growlers from Grumble Street. It's strange but true that many people actually enjoy talking defeat. And misery loves company.

Remember, on Praise Avenue, there's no room for gloom. You can avoid the gloom-trap by repeating this verse to yourself at the beginning of each new day: *"This is the day which the Lord hath made; we will rejoice and be glad in it"* (Psalm 118:24). It is a fact that the Lord makes each new day especially for us. Whatever God makes is good, and good for us. Genesis 1:31 tells us that *"...God saw everything that he had made, and, behold, it was very good."* Since the Lord made the day, it's a day for good living, not grumbling. He expects us to rejoice and be glad. *"Serve the Lord with gladness,"* not sadness, commands Psalm 100. Say these words: "The Lord made this day for me. I shall be glad and rejoice."

As long as God is for you, with you, and within you, there's absolutely no room for gloom! God isn't a gloomy God, and He doesn't want gloomy children!

The Bible commands us, *"Neither give place to the devil"* (Ephesians 4:27). When you give place to gloom in your life, you're giving place to the Devil. He is the author of gloom. So make it your glad declaration: "In my life, there's no room for gloom! Hallelujah!"

There are so many of God's children who are in low spirits. They're depressed and disgusted with life. But they don't need to stay that way. If you feel this way, right now, walk out of your slough of despondency. Put a sudden stop to sulking! Certainly, life has much to dampen the spirit. But you are living by God's Word! Do not sink to the level of the pessimistic crowd. Quit wearing that long face. Your Lord is alive! He is risen! Shout Hallelujahs! Be a sparkling person, with no room for pouting, fretting, or a dreary existence. Praise the Lord often. Count your blessings at bedtime, and you will be surprised at all the Lord has done for you throughout the day.

Let me emphasize again that one of the most important passages in the Bible that will help dispel gloom is Isaiah 41:10: *"Fear thou not; for I am with thee: be not dismayed; for I am thy God: I will strengthen thee; yea, I will help thee; yea, I will uphold thee with the right hand of my righteousness."* How can you be down when God is holding you up?

I am reminded of the story of a particularly fierce battle that Napoleon once fought. During the heat of the battle, Napoleon decided that victory was impossible. Calling one of his drummers he told him to go out and sound a call for retreat. The drummer, with a twinkle in his eye, replied that he didn't know how to sound a retreat, but that he'd be glad to sound an advance.

Feeling just a little ashamed, Napoleon saw his error and told the lad to go ahead and sound the advance. He did, and the army won the victory, even though the circumstances seemed to spell out certain defeat.

If only every Christian would refuse to talk defeat! What victory we would have! This is why we are instructed in God's Word to give praise to Him in all things. God is trying to tell us that our day-to-day victory will be only as great as we are willing to make it. Each day, we must discipline ourselves to forget the call to retreat, and to sound the praise-call to victory. Praise is the only workable way to advance and conquer.

Over the years, I have found that many Christians are what I call "part-time praisers". This type of Christian makes a habit of praising God in prayer meetings and church services; but when he gets out into the world, he usually goes along and grumbles in agreement with every other grumbler he meets. Friend, it is not God's will that we be part-time residents of Praise Avenue. When God tells us to praise Him in all things, then that is exactly what we are supposed to do. The Bible does not tell us to praise God part of the time, or in some things; rather, it tells us to praise God in all things.

I wish that every Christian would carry this message out into the world. What a sweet mission of mercy it would be to carry the sound of victory to the bad-mouths of the world!

A man I know once said, "There is victory in praise, and there is praise in victory." How true that is! Such was the case with Stephen, the first Christian to be martyred. Stephen was falsely accused of blasphemy, and was hauled outside of Jerusalem to be stoned to death. Just as he was about to die, he prayed, *"Lord, lay not this sin to their charge"* (Acts 7:60). What a victorious prayer! No complaining here! No self-pity! No gloom! Only love, peace, and joy!

Do you want to lead the victorious life? Do you want to see defeat defeated? You can, my friend, if only you act upon the Word of God. Here's what to do:

1. Don't say, "I can't." The phrase, "I can't," is nowhere in the Bible. Speak God's language. Say what His Word says. Harmonize with heaven by affirming Gods Word. Agree with God by agreeing with His Word: *"I can*

do all things through Christ which strengtheneth me"
(Philippians 4:13).

2. Don't say, "I can't receive my healing." Instead, boldly
say, "I can receive my healing, for *'with His stripes we are
healed'* (Isaiah 53:5). I can receive my healing because
Jesus said, *'They shall lay hands on the sick, and they shall
recover'* (Mark 16:18). Hands have been laid upon me;
thus, I am recovering."

3. Don't say, "I can't pay my bills." Rather, declare it
emphatically, "I can pay my bills, for *'my God shall supply
all* [my] *need according to his riches in glory by Christ
Jesus'* (Philippians 4:19). I have honored the Lord by
paying my tithes and giving offerings in His name, and
He says, *'I will...open you the windows of heaven, and
pour you out a blessing...and I will rebuke the devourer
for your sakes'* (Malachi 3:10, 11)."

4. Don't say, "I can't witness in power, because I'm not
a good speaker." Defeat that negative statement by
affirming, "I can witness in power, for I have received
the Holy Spirit into my life, and Jesus said, *'ye shall
receive power, after that the Holy Ghost is come upon
you'* (Acts 1:8). I can share my testimony, my witness
for Christ, and the message of His salvation because
I am energized by the mighty Holy Ghost from
heaven."

5. Don't say, "I just can't get my prayers answered." This
kind of expression will close the heavens to your life.
With assurance, speak out, "I can receive the answer
to my prayers, for Jesus said, *'Whatsoever ye shall ask
the Father in my name, he will give it you'* (John 16:23). I
can receive mighty answers from God, for He said, *'Call
unto me, and I will answer thee, and shew thee great and*

mighty things...' (Jeremiah 33:3). I know I can receive the answer to my prayers, for *'this is the confidence that we have in him, that, if we ask any thing according to his will, he heareth us'* (1 John 5:14)."

6. Don't say, "I can't see my loved ones won to Jesus Christ." That's a lie of the Devil, and for you to speak it is to give place to the Devil. Agree with God's promise and declare it: "I can see my loved ones won to Jesus Christ, for the Bible says, *'Believe on the Lord Jesus Christ, and thou shalt be saved, and thy house'* (Acts 16:31). I shall never fear that my loved ones will be lost forever in hell. I can see all my loved ones saved because I am God's instrument to pray and believe for their salvation."

7. Don't say, "I can't overcome my overeating." Remember that God said, *"My grace is sufficient for thee"* (2 Corinthians 12:9). Therefore you can say, "Through God's grace, I can resist overeating. I can, by Christ's grace, overcome being a compulsive eater, and eat with moderation and temperance. I have discovered the secret: I can conquer my problem through the grace of my Lord Jesus Christ."

Do you see? God wants you to quit talking gloom, be a praiser, and live in victory.

TWELVE

WHAT MONEY CRUNCH?

The knocking continued as I hurried to the front door. When I finally opened it, I was met by a lean, businesslike man with a well-set jaw.

"I'm here to collect your car payment," he announced flatly.

My heart sank for a moment as I told him that we didn't have the money to meet the payment right then.

"Well, then," the man said, "I have no other choice but to take the car."

"Oh, that can't happen," I pleaded. "We need that car. Besides, I've never had that happen, and I just won't have that. Will you go back to your company and request a five-day extension? You could phone, but we don't have one. I'm sure that I can get the money within five days."

The man hesitated for a moment. His face seemed to soften. "All right," he said pessimistically. "It so happens that I'm on my way back to the office now.

I'll see what I can do about getting an extension for you. But don't get your hopes up. I'm almost certain they won't go along with it."

"How soon will you be back?" I asked anxiously. "Sometime this afternoon—likely to repossess the car!"

I watched the man go down the walk. As he started to get into his car, he looked over the top and yelled, "You'd better get your personal stuff out of that thing before I get back. I won't have time to wait." With that note, he got into his car and drove off.

My wife had left for a funeral only minutes before. I was caring for our four small children. So I was left to face this situation alone.

Quickly, I had to make a decision. I looked out at the car in front of our house. Should I go out and clean out the personal contents? No, I wouldn't do that.

Then another decision had to be made—without delay. Either I could panic, resign to failure, and watch the car be taken away, or else, I could turn my faith to God, and trust in Him with my whole heart.

I'll admit that I was tempted to doubt. But my wife and I had been nourishing our hearts on God's Word, and the truth of Philippians 4:19 flashed to my mind: *"But my God shall supply all your need according to his riches in glory by Christ Jesus."*

I made my decision: I would practice what I had been preaching. I would dare to confess God's Word aloud. I would not waver in my faith. I would not yield to the evidence of my senses. (The senses always war against the Word: I "heard" the man say he would likely have to repossess my car. I could "feel" deep anxiety about this urgent matter. My imagination told me I would soon "see" the car taken away from me.)

But God's Word was above the evidence of the senses. His truth was superior to natural truth. I would take my stand boldly with God's Word.

I began saying over and over, "My God shall supply all of my need." (See Philippians 4:19.) I kept on saying it with courage and conviction.

As this Scripture fell from my lips, my heart was beginning to agree. My confidence was rising. In a short time, I was shouting it: "My God shall supply all of my need!" It gushed forth like a fountain in my spirit. "My God shall supply all of my need!" I said it over and over. It was not a song of desperation or unbelief. It was a song of sheer joy. I knew it was gloriously true.

As I continued to confess this Scripture aloud, coupling it with joyful praises, I could almost "feel" the money in my pocket! The Word alone generated this kind of awareness.

While I was yet confessing, praising, and singing, another knock came on my front door. When I opened it, there stood a taxi driver.

"Since the office was unable to reach you by phone, I was sent here to inform you that there is a money order at the telegraph office for you. If you will come down and sign for it, you can receive the money," the taxi driver politely stated. (Our town was so small that the taxi drivers often delivered messages for Western Union.) I thanked him for this message and assured him I would be down to the telegraph office to claim the money as soon as I could.

After watching him pull away from the curb, I closed the door and began praising the Lord again. I just knew that it was Him alone who acted on someone, somewhere, to send me that money. As I stood there praising the Lord for His faithfulness, I heard yet another knock at the door.

When I opened the door, I was met by the bill collector, and another man whom I assumed was coming to drive away our car.

Before either man had a chance to say a word, I smiled at them and said, "Listen, fellows, I know where I can get the money right now. There's just one problem though; I'm watching our four little children while my wife is at a funeral. If you two gentlemen wouldn't mind watching the kids for me, I can be back with the money in a few minutes."

Both men glanced at each other, and looked a bit hesitant. Finally, the collector spoke up. "Okay, sure, I guess we could stay with the kids. It's a bit unusual—but if you can get the money, then why not? Just hurry it up."

My heart was by now fairly bursting with praise, as I pulled on my coat. I had the money; I had free baby-sitters; I had everything I needed!

When I arrived at the telegraph office, there was the wire. My heavenly Father spoke to a man over six hundred miles away to send me one hundred fifty dollars—almost twice the amount needed for the car payment.

Later, I found out that this man first thought that he would send the money through the mail, but the Spirit impressed him to wire it to me. The amazing thing is that the very time when he was led to wire it to me was the same moment that I started praising God for my situation!

It never occurred to me until later that, in the natural, I did a rather dangerous thing to leave the children with those two strangers. But, then, the babysitters God provides are bound to be reliable, aren't they? And I still maintain that there's nothing to fear when God is in control.

At any rate, I learned that those who live on Praise Avenue are showered with the best of heaven's blessings. Praising God in the midst of flat bank accounts and hard times opens the windows of heaven and keeps you happy in Jesus.

How well I remember the bills that piled up during my wife's sickness! Stricken with rheumatic fever, she was so sick that I finally had to leave the field of evangelism in order to care for my family. I couldn't leave my wife alone in that condition, nor did I have the money to hire someone to stay with her.

Weeks passed, and there was no income. I mortgaged our furniture, but soon that money was used up, and I had no money left at all. Still, I determined to keep praising the Lord.

During this time of dire poverty and hardship, I was exploring God's Word like never before, hoping to find some answer to our problem. Then one day I happened to turn to 2 Corinthians 9:6–8, and there God spoke to me in a way that I'll never forget:

> But this I say, He which soweth sparingly shall reap also sparingly; and he which soweth bountifully shall reap also bountifully. Every man according as he purposeth in his heart, so let him give; not grudgingly or of necessity: for God loveth a cheerful giver. And God is able to make all grace abound toward you; that ye, always having all sufficiency in all things, may abound to every good work.

Words cannot describe the feeling that I had when I read that passage. Here, Paul was describing God's plan for man's spiritual and financial prosperity. As I read the passage, I noticed that there were three major points in his message.

First, we reap what we sow. If we plant a little, we reap a little. If we plant a great deal; we reap a great deal. When I thought about our poverty, I realized that this passage threw the responsibility right back at me. If I was reaping very little income, it was just because I hadn't been "planting" enough.

Then Paul emphasized that we must be cheerful in our giving. God wants His children to "plant" their money with praise and thanksgiving, not with a grudging heart.

Finally, Paul pointed out that when God gives us extra financial blessings, He wants us to share them with those who are less fortunate, so that they too will thank Him for His goodness.

Well, after I read that passage from 2 Corinthians, I promised God that I would be a generous giver if He would supply us with something to give. And He did exactly that. After being without a single dollar of income for more than a month, I finally received five dollars through the mail. It came from a friend whom God moved to share our burden. Cheerfully, and with praise in my heart, I gave the Lord a generous portion of that money.

Immediately, God moved on the scene again. A woman whom I never met from Evanston, Illinois, sent me twenty-five dollars. I wrote her to thank her for her gift. When she replied, she sent me a money order for a hundred dollars!

Praising the Lord even more, I gave a good portion of these amounts to the Lord's work also. Sure enough, the Lord continued blessing us, both financially and spiritually.

Then came the unforgettable Sunday evening when the Lord healed my wife as I read to her the Twenty-seventh Psalm. She boldly got out of her bed, stood up, and confessed, "The Lord is the strength of my life."

Although the Lord beautifully healed my wife that Sunday, there was a period recovery that naturally followed. Meanwhile, my dear mother and dad came from Oregon to care for our children. That freed me to return to the ministry.

For ten consecutive months, I received a hundred-dollar money order from that dear woman in Evanston. I praised God for every cent of that money, gave away a portion of all she gave me, and gradually got caught up on my bills.

Now, I could have just played safe and used all that money for my bills. A lot of us are tempted to do that at times, aren't we? An old story from the Deep South illustrates this very clearly. It seems that a ragged farmer was standing on the steps of his tumbledown shack when a stranger stopped by for a drink of water.

"How's your cotton coming along?" the stranger inquired.

"Ain't got none," replied the farmer.

"Did you plant any?" asked the stranger.

"Nope," was the reply. "'Fraid o' boll weevils."

"Well," continued the visitor, "how's your corn?"

"Didn't plant none," came the answer. "'Fraid there wasn't goin' to be no rain."

The visitor persevered. "Well, how are your potatoes?"

"Ain't got none—scared of the potato bugs."

"Really, what did you plant?" pressed the stranger. "Nothin'," was the calm reply. "I jest played it safe." Perhaps some of us have been "playing safe" with our money. And God will permit us to do that, if that's what we choose. We can keep it all for ourselves. But if we want to reap a good harvest of blessings, then we need to plant in faith—and water with praise. That's the way to prosperity—both spiritual and material.

THIRTEEN

HANDLING HOPELESS SITUATIONS

Probably my greatest experience in living the praise life came one spring. I organized a group of people to travel to the Holy Land with me.

When we arrived in Montreal, Quebec, we found that the tour company we were working with had gone bankrupt. As tour leader, I found myself with the embarrassing responsibility of informing our group that we must contribute more cash if we intended to continue our journey. Thus, it was that I had to spend my only two hundred dollars in traveler's checks. This left me with the rather unenviable total fortune of sixteen dollars and seventy-one cents!

As I sat there in the airport, I pulled out my wallet and began recounting my assets. I felt on the verge of despair. Just how was I to travel halfway around the world with sixteen dollars and seventy-one cents? The thought hardly passed through my mind when the Lord whispered softly to my heart, "Just praise Me and see." It was that simple.

As I began praising the Lord for the situation, I felt a release from my burden. Suddenly, I knew that the Lord would take care of me. Things might appear to be a bit grim, but God would still keep everything under control.

Flying over the Atlantic Ocean, I couldn't help but feel a twinge of excitement. It was almost like being a child on Christmas Eve again. I knew that God had surprises in store for me; I just didn't know what they were.

The surprise that finally came, however, was a little more than the group and I were counting on. Due to scheduling problems, we were divided into three groups. Imagine my surprise when I found out that one of the groups consisted of only one person—me!

When I arrived in Zurich, I hurried to be reunited with my suitcase which contained almost every item of clothing I owned. Words can never describe the feeling I had when an apologetic Swiss official told me that my suitcase had been accidentally shipped back to Canada. If you've ever had a similar experience, you'd know how I felt.

At the same time, I thought, "This is ridiculous! I'm the victim of carelessness. I'll tell those incompetent officials just what I think of their blunder!"

As I was turning over in my mind just exactly what I would tell those people, the Holy Spirit checked me with this thought: "But you're the man who goes around preaching about the power of praise." I rebelled for a moment. "Sure," I thought, "but I'm almost ten thousand miles away from home; nobody knows me here. I guess I could be a hypocrite and get away with it."

I was just beginning to weigh the word "hypocrite" when I felt the voice of the Holy Spirit replying, "It is true that nobody here knows you, but I know you, and I am watching you."

With that, He won.

I looked up and softly said, "Thank you, Lord; You're still in control of my life, my clothes—everything!"

As I stood there silently praising the Lord, I was reminded of the passage of Scripture in Isaiah 61:3 where the Lord promises to give us *"the garment of praise for the spirit of heaviness."* As I pondered the meaning of "the garment of praise," I decided that if that was what the Lord wanted me to wear, then that was fine with me. Even if my clothes were half a world away, I could still wear the "garment of praise."

Incredibly, even though the clothes I had on was all I had to wear for the next sixteen consecutive days, that suit stayed neat and looked as if it had been freshly pressed all during the journey. All I did was put on the "garment of praise" every day, and the Lord kept me on top in every way.

As my plane left for Rome and Beirut, I wondered what else would be in store for me on my journey. Throughout the trip, I reminded myself of the text of Philippians 4:19: *"But my God shall supply all your need according to his riches in glory by Christ Jesus."* Thus, you can be sure I was ready for a miracle that evening when I arrived in Beirut, Lebanon, with only a dime in my pocket!

The Lebanese customs official who was trying to take care of me, but I didn't understand English, and unfortunately, I didn't understand so much as a single word of Arabic. As the two of us stood there gesturing at each other, a kindly gentleman from Alitalia Airlines stepped up.

"Perhaps I could help you, Sir," he said.

I hardly told him half of my story, when he interrupted: "Sir, allow me to make you the guest of Alitalia Airlines!"

The guest of Alitalia Airlines! I could hardly believe my ears. Who? Me? Why? (I could think of no reason for this—unless they were trying to compensate for having lost my bags.) God was indeed working a miracle—and what a miracle it turned out to be! The airline provided me with the most luxurious hotel accommodations that I ever experienced. To top it off, they provided me with all of my meals at no charge!

Now that I was in Beirut, I knew my problem would soon be solved. My wife promised to wire some money from home, so all I had to do was find some way to get to a bank and pick up the money. So, on Friday morning, I hailed a taxi and explained my situation to the driver.

"Sir," I told him, "I don't have any money to pay my fare, but I want you to take me to the Chase Manhattan Bank where I do have money that has been wired to me."

The driver agreed to my request and took me up and down the hills of Beirut to the bank. We arrived at the door only to find that it was closed. The driver was visibly shaken. "Sir," he said, "I forgot. This is Good Friday and the bank is closed."

I was probably just as shaken as the driver, only not as visibly.

I breathed a quick word of prayer and then asked the driver to take me to the Royal Jordanian Airlines, since they were flying me to Jerusalem.

As I sat there in the seat of the cab, I was silently praying, "Lord, what should I do?"

The trip to the Airlines really stalled the driver while I waited on the Lord for an answer.

As the cab rounded the next bend in the road, I suddenly felt the Lord telling me to go to the House of Tours, the agency which coordinates many Holy Land tours.

The cab driver agreed. Since I owed him several dollars already, he wasn't about to let me out of his sight! I had the feeling that he was considering taking my coat for his fare!

When we finally arrived at the House of Tours, I introduced myself to the gentlemen in charge. They immediately recognized my name as being the organizer of a tour from Canada.

The taxi driver was by now an inseparable companion, for he was a man desperate for his fare! I'll never forget the expression of relief that passed over his face when one of the men from the Tours Company paid my fare.

After the driver left, I sat down in the seat offered me and quietly said, "Thank You, Jesus. You're leading me one step at a time."

Still praising the Lord in my heart, I briefly discussed my predicament with the men from the Tours Company. They explained to me how it was imperative that I leave immediately to join my group in Jerusalem. I explained to them that I had a travel ticket, but no money.

One of the men asked, "How much do you need?"

I replied, "Perhaps fifty dollars."

"Fifty dollars!" they replied in unison. "You'll need more than that!"

"Well," I said, "maybe two hundred dollars would be better.

Again, they thought that was too little.

I sat there amazed that two perfect strangers were preparing to loan me so much money when they knew nothing more about me than what they heard from my fellow tour members from Canada.

Finally, one of the men spoke up. "Mr. Gossett, we will loan you five hundred dollars to get you on your way."

"Five hundred dollars!" It was my turn to be shocked. My heart fairly soared. God had answered my praises.

Late that night, I arrived in Jordan. As I rode the fifty miles to Jerusalem, my heart was beating rapidly; to think that I was now in the land of my Lord! To me, it was a moving experience just to be there.

Five of our tour members were in the lobby fellowshipping when I arrived at the hotel. When they saw me—after searching vainly for me for days—they were astonished. One of them later told me that she was almost as shocked as the disciples were that night when they saw Jesus walking on the water. I was, I suppose, just as surprised—not at being able to be there—but at how the Lord arranged it. But I still think that God wouldn't have done such a beautiful series of miracles if I hadn't decided to praise and thank Him in all things.

I can see now that my move to Praise Avenue was one of the most important moves of my life. Like other praisers, I soon saw that true praise not only changed my outlook on "bad" situations, but often caused the situation itself to change.

When we praise God, "*we know that all things work together for good to them that love God*" (Romans 8:28). When we turn a situation over to the Lord, we permit Him to work things out for the best.

One of the best illustrations of this principle is found in the book of Acts. It is the story of Paul and Silas, two of the best-known residents on Praise Avenue.

Paul and Silas had just been thrown into the jail in Philippi on false charges. It had been several hours since they were flogged, and their backs were torn and swollen. Their feet were in hard, brutal stocks. Every movement brought added pain. By all of the world's standards, these men had every right to complain.

Did they though? Absolutely not. But neither did they just sit there, wishing that they were out of their "bad" situation. Instead, they decided to sing hymns and praise God. God responded to the praises of Paul and Silas. The Bible tells us that "*suddenly there was a great earthquake, so that the foundations of the prison were shaken: and immediately all the doors were opened, and every one's bands were loosed*" (Acts 16:26).

God isn't one to go halfway. The Bible goes on to tell us that because of this miracle, the jailer and his entire family were converted!

All of this goes to prove that God can, and will, change even the most hopeless situation, if we will just hold it up to Him in praise.

No situation is truly hopeless. Down through the centuries, Christians have found that nothing is impossible with God. Many years ago, an unknown saint wrote the following lines:

> In the days before passenger trains were equipped with lights, I was traveling by rail to a distant city. Our route was through several tunnels; consequently, at times the cars would be enveloped in deep darkness. Beside me sat a sympathetic Englishman. We were enjoying a pleasant conversation when we started into a long, underground mountain pass, and it became pitch black in our coach. My companion, a Christian, had traveled that way many times before. Reassuringly he said, 'Cheer up, my friend, we're not in a sack—there's a 'ole at the other end!' I never forgot his words. They cheered me later in many of the dark passages of life.

So praise Him! No matter how dark the tunnel, you can make it through with praise. And when we are willing to go all the way in our praises to the Lord, the Lord will be more than willing to go all the way in response. Only then can we expect really great miracles to happen.

FOURTEEN

SEVENTY TIMES SEVEN

Not too long ago, while I was in Los Angeles, a woman came to me after a meeting and said, "Don, God has put His finger on the things in my life that are standing between me and Him. Ever since I married, my in-laws have been making life as miserable as possible for me. I've come to the point where I almost hate them. Don, I know this isn't right, but I don't know what to do about it."

This woman was so sincere, that everything within me wanted to help her.

I explained to her how Jesus said that His grace would be sufficient strength in such situations, and that we only need to ask Him to help us.

As we prayed to God for the Lord's strength in that situation, tears flowed down her cheeks. She told the Lord how bitter she felt, and she earnestly asked Him to help her.

As soon as she paused in her prayer, I suggested that she try praising God for her in-laws.

For a moment, she seemed to rebel at that idea. Finally, though, she reached the place where she cried out, "Lord, I thank You and praise You for my in-laws, and Lord, I can and I will and I do forgive them!"

What a joy it was to see this woman lay her burden at the foot of the cross!

Two days later, she came back to tell me what happened.

She went immediately to her in-laws' home after we talked, and with a heart full of praise, talked to them. As she talked in this attitude of praise, Jesus filled her heart with love for her in-laws.

She told them of all the bitterness that she had felt towards them, and how she wanted them to forgive her.

When it was all over, she and her in-laws were reconciled, and both sides felt closer than they ever felt before.

I'm convinced that one of the most priceless possessions of the people on Praise Avenue is the power to forgive. You can't buy this power with an amount of money, but it's yours for the asking when you learn to praise God for people who've offended you.

Unforgiveness is like cancer. It starts out as a small speck within us; but when allowed to grow, it ends up as a large, ugly tumor that all but stops our spiritual growth.

In San Francisco, a little Chinese lady told me emphatically that it was useless for her to come to me for a healing if, first of all, she had to forgive everyone. She said there was a certain man who caused her much physical and mental torture, and she refused to forgive him. It saddened me to see that poor soul left that meeting without her physical and spiritual healing.

I often wonder who is hurt more in such cases—the person who holds grudge, or the person who committed the wrong. In almost every case, I think that it is the person who holds the grudge, whose soul is filled with bitterness, who is the one who suffers the greater loss. I have seen many cases like this, where people harbor the spirit of unforgiveness to such a point that they actually allow Satan to make them physically ill.

Over the years, I have found that the easiest way to keep a right attitude towards God and those around me is to keep praising Him when others do me wrong. As long as I keep doing this, I find that the grudges simply vanish. What a relief it is to be able to be set free from the burdens of unforgiveness!

Now you can actually enjoy this freedom as long as you choose to. The Bible makes it clear that forgiveness is not an occasional responsibility. Rather, through Jesus, we are to extend constant forgiveness to those who wrong us.

Peter, when he came to Jesus, asked him, *"Lord, how oft shall my brother sin against me, and I forgive him? Till seven times?"* (Matthew 18:21).

Then we read that Jesus said to him, *"I say not unto thee, until seven times: but, until seventy times seven"* (verse 22).

Now let's first look at the question Peter asked, and then the answer he proposed; both of them are very interesting. The question is, "How often shall I forgive?" How many times must I let a man walk all over me without retaliating? When can I say, "Well, Mister, you've gone just too far this time?" That's the question: "How many times must I forgive, Lord? Seven times?"

Now some would look down their nose at Peter and criticize him for saying that. The fact is that most Christians, if provoked seven times in a row, would grow quite angry. Indeed, I think that many Christians would hardly tolerate provocation two or three times.

But then we come to Jesus' answer: "No, not seven times—but seventy times seven!"

"Lord," we're tempted to say, "do you really mean that? Do you mean that I'm just to forgive and forgive and forgive? Do you mean that I'm never to retaliate? Do you mean I'm not to stand up for my rights when people take advantage of me?"

"Yes," says the Lord. "That's what I mean. Forgive—seventy times seven times, if necessary."

Martin Luther passed down an old story which illustrates the matter beautifully. According to his story, two mountain goats met each other on a narrow ledge just wide enough for one of the animals. On the left, there was a sheer drop-off, and on the right, a deep lake.

The two goats stood there facing each other. What should they do? They couldn't back up; that would be too dangerous. They couldn't turn around; the ledge was too narrow.

Now if the goats didn't have any more sense than some people, they would have met head-on and started butting each other till they fell into the lake below. But Luther says that goats have better sense than people. He says that one of them will lie down on the trail and let the other literally walk over him—and both will be safe. But they must be willing (at least one of them) to humbly lie down and let the other pass over him. If they were like some of us, they would stand and argue about who should lie down and who should walk over. But sometimes goats are more sensible than people.

But someone will say, "You mean I'm to let people walk all over me if they want to?" Well, it's better to do that than to put up with the misery of a grudge.

Jesus gave us a good reason to forgive. While on the Mount of the Beatitudes, he told the crowd, *"Judge not, and ye shall not be judged: condemn not, and ye shall not be condemned: forgive, and ye shall be forgiven"* (Luke 6:37).

How comforting it is for those whose capacity for forgiveness is great, to know that Jesus will forgive us in like manner!

But what if our capacity for forgiveness is less than it should be? What if we're less than perfect? (And that covers all of us.) What should we do? My suggestion is that we try praising God for the person or group that is irritating us. We could start out by praising God for the person who is the most offensive to us. Why? Because we know that God can make even that person a real blessing to us if we'll just praise Him and accept the blessing He sends.

Probably, the best illustration of this principle was given by Jesus Himself. In answer to Peter's question about forgiveness, He told this parable:

> *Therefore is the kingdom of heaven likened unto a certain king, which would take account of his servants. And when he had begun to reckon, one was brought unto him, which owed him ten thousand talents. But forasmuch as he had not to pay, his lord commanded him to be sold, and his wife, and children, and all that he had, and payment to be made. The servant therefore fell down, and worshipped him, saying, Lord, have patience with me, and I will pay thee all. Then the lord of that servant was moved with compassion, and loosed him, and forgave him the debt. But when the same servant went out, and found one of his fellow servants, which owed him an hundred pence: and he laid hands on him, and took him by the throat, saying, Pay me that thou owest. And his fellow servant fell down at his feet, and besought him, saying, Have patience with me, and I will pay thee all. And he would not: but went and cast him into prison, till he should pay the debt. So when his fellow servants saw what was done, they were very sorry, and came and told unto their lord all that was done. Then his lord, after that he had called him, said unto him, O thou wicked servant, I forgave thee all that debt, because thou desiredst me: Shouldest not thou also have had compassion on thy fellow servant, even as I had pity on thee? And his lord was wroth, and delivered him to the tormentors, till he should pay all that was due unto him. So likewise shall my heavenly Father do also unto you, if ye from your hearts forgive not everyone his brother their trespasses.* (Matthew 18:23–35)

A friend of mine once said, "Praise helps forgiveness, but unforgiveness hinders praise." How true that is! If you find yourself fitting into the second half of that little quote, then I suggest you take the following steps immediately:

First, ask the Lord to help you to genuinely forgive the person or group that has wronged you. Ask God to give you His love for that person or group.

Second, ask God to help you forget the past. Ask Him to fill your heart with joy, peace, and praise.

Third, take a deliberate step to praise God for the person or group that wronged you. Don't act on your feelings. Forgiveness is not a matter of how you feel so much as it is a matter of what you do. Act upon the Word of God. Praise God, and keep on praising Him for that person until you feel the peace of God.

Fourth, if possible or practical, go to the person who wronged you, and in Jesus' love, let him know that you forgive him. You may be surprised to find that he didn't even know that he did anything to hurt you.

Last of all, ask the Lord to help you get back into the regular praise-life. Your fellowship with God will become sweet again as you continue praising Him.

If you follow these steps, you will truly have something to praise God for, since you will know all is well between you and your brother, and that God the Father forgives you as you forgave your brother.

Now, isn't that something to praise God for?

FIFTEEN

A GOSSETT
IS A GOSSETT?

My mind still smarts at the thought of that day in my boyhood when I first decided that I wanted to be baptized into Christ's family. Mustering all the courage I had, I approached a deacon, who promptly presented me to the church's pastor.

"Pastor, this is Donald Gossett," the deacon announced. "He is thirteen years old. He wants to be baptized in water and join our church."

I knew the pastor would be happy about that. I expected him to break into a big smile. I expected the deacon to put his arm around me and praise the Lord for the change in my life. But, instead, the deacon added, "Donald's father owns the pool hall, and his mother and father have that tavern called the Highway Cafe. His father also owns that gambling place on South Broadway."

As the deacon was giving me this introduction, I dropped my head in shame. I was fighting to keep the tears back. I didn't want this pastor to know what my dad did for a living. My coming to Christ and wanting to follow Him in water baptism and church membership was my sincere effort to discover a better life than I knew in the past.

I had been born again in that church at the age of twelve. As I continued to attend services, I heard the older Christians speaking of water baptism and the importance of joining the church. I decided that if these two steps would make me a better Christian, then I wanted to take them.

At first, I knew very few people in the large church. Later, though, I became acquainted with a deacon—the only person in leadership that I knew.

It was to this deacon that I had gone one evening at the close of the service to inquire about what I had to do to be baptized and join the church. He took me to meet the pastor, and that's when he gave the introduction that so embarrassed me as a shy, timid, fearful young fellow of thirteen years.

The pastor kindly replied, "Donald, we will present your name to our church board for consideration. We will let you know."

I thanked him with my head still bowed, and made a quick exit out of that church. As I walked home alone in the dark, my heart was broken. Why did that deacon have to say that? Was there no way to escape from the fact that my dad was a sinner? Did my dad's business life always have to involve me? I was branded! My dad's life and business would probably always mark me as being from a "bad class." After all, a Gossett is a Gossett.

There was no way out for me, I thought. Going back to that church, or any other church, was useless. I made a firm decision. I would never go back to church again.

For nearly three years, I didn't return to any church services. I still had a spiritual hunger for God and the Bible. I feebly said my prayers each night, and read the Word even though I didn't understand it. I desperately needed teaching, but I felt that there were no teachers who wanted me around.

It was a long time before I realized that the deacon didn't mean to hurt me. But, oh, how it would have helped if he just praised God for me instead of reminding me of my family's reputation!

Didn't he understand that I didn't want to be like the rest of the Gossetts? Didn't he know how he was hurting me—a babe in Christ? Didn't he know how tender I was?

Oh, my friends, if one of your Christian brothers or sisters is but a babe in Christ, don't offend him by unkind remarks. It matters not what his past record is, if he is one of Jesus' redeemed, do not hurt him.

"But," you say, "Jerry is a thief."

No, that isn't true.

"Oh, but it is," you reply. "Jerry has been convicted of theft twice. So it's a fact—Jerry is a thief."

No, your reasoning is incorrect. You see, when you say that Jerry is a thief, you're saying that Jerry has stolen (which may be true) and that Jerry will steal again. But you don't know that he will steal again, do you? You cannot discount what a man is now on the basis of his past record. And nobody ought to understand that better than a Christian. Surely you understand what a change Christ can make in a man in a split second! You know that Christ can take a man who has stolen and change him so that he'll never steal again.

And yet we sometimes hear even Christian people saying, "Well, a crook is a crook—and if he gypped me once, he'll do it again." But how unfair! Would you want anyone to judge you on the basis of what you were ten years ago? Twenty years ago? Thirty or forty years ago? Or, if you're a brand new convert, even on the basis of what you were last week? No, when you learn to think like Jesus thinks, then you know that a man may change in a moment—and you dare not judge him on the basis of his past. We must accept him as he is now, and praise God for him.

This is the way Jesus thought of people. No matter what kind of persons he met, he was always willing to accept them when they came to him. Tax collectors, liars, cheats, adulterers, robbers—they were all received alike by Jesus. Never did He say to anyone, "Go clean up your past, and then I'll accept you." No, he accepted them as they were, and then proceeded to work changes in them as needed.

You see, we Christians have a lot of kinks in our thinking. Just because we've been born again doesn't mean that all of our thinking has been straightened out. We must learn to think as Jesus thinks—and I'm sure that's what Paul meant in Romans 12:2 when he said, "*And be not conformed to this world but be ye transformed by the renewing of your mind, that ye may prove what is that good, and acceptable, and perfect, will of God.*" The renewing of the mind is one of the biggest challenges that face Christians. But if you listen to what the Holy Spirit says to you in this chapter, you can make some real headway in your Christian growth, and learn how to praise God for other people.

A lot of us have difficulty praising God for our neighbors on Praise Avenue because we can't forget their past:

Fifteen years ago, Sally Jones was untrue to her husband. And although she has straightened out, been saved, moved onto Praise Avenue, and is getting along fine with her husband, still, in the minds of some people, she will never be anything else but a street-walker.

Or, perhaps the problem is right in your own family. Back when you and your wife first got married, she wasn't too good at handling money. And even though she has learned a lot since those days, you still keep reminding her about how wasteful she is.

Oh, my Christian friends, how we need to start praising God for one another instead of digging up the miserable past!

Sometimes we offend people by "pigeon-holing" them, assuming that certain groups of people are all alike. If we notice that Mr.

Reuben has a knack for making money, we sometimes make comments like, "Well, a Jew's a Jew, there's no getting around that!" This is just another way of saying that all Jews are alike: they all have their fingers in the money. And yet, if you stop to think about that, you know that isn't true. Jew #1 isn't the same as Jew #2 or Jew #3. It isn't clear thinking or Christian thinking to say, "A Jew is a Jew."

Of course, there are many other groups besides Jews who suffer such offenses. We may say, "A woman driver is a woman driver"— which is supposed to mean that they're all very poor drivers. Or, we may say, "A redhead is a redhead"—which is supposed to mean that they all have bad tempers. And this is exactly the way we offend a lot of young Christians. We lump people together and fail to take into account their individual differences. You see, young Christian #1 is not young Christian #2. Redhead #1 is not redhead #2. Woman driver #1 is not woman driver #2. Gossett #1 is not Gossett #2.

How glad I am to testify that before I turned sixteen, a "religious emphasis week" was conducted in our high school. The preacher spoke right to my heart.

The Holy Spirit used his message to bring me back to God and to all-out Christian living. I went back to church and was water baptized.

Often, though, I've shuddered to think what might have happened if I allowed that deacon's verbal offense to keep me away from the Christian life.

Friends, we must be careful never to be guilty of possessing a smug, self-righteous attitude toward others.

I have found that when we encounter people who we might be tempted to look down on, it is always best to praise God for them. When we praise God for someone, we are taking the same kind of attitude toward that person that God takes.

We are taking an attitude of love. When we praise God for those who God places in our path, we are sharing in God's love. And we can communicate His love to that person.

I have often thought that my parents might have been won to the Lord sooner had it not been for an over-zealous Christian woman who failed to keep her heart full of loving praise.

My parents accompanied me to a service one night after I came back to the Lord. A personal worker came to our seat during the invitation.

"Are you a Christian?" she asked me.

I quietly assured her that I was.

Then she turned to my parents and asked them the same question. When my parents replied that they hadn't accepted the Lord, this woman proceeded to scold them: "Aren't you ashamed of yourselves? Your son is a Christian, and you're not! Come on and be saved tonight," she reprimanded, with a scowl on her face.

At the time, my parents were under conviction and feeling their need of the Lord. But the censorious attitude of that woman repelled them. How much more effective she might have been had she said something like, "Oh, how I praise the Lord that the two of you are here, and how I praise the Lord that He loves you!"

That's the way to be happy on Praise Avenue. Praise the Lord for everybody. In this way, you'll not only keep the joy of the Lord in your own heart, but you'll spread happiness everywhere you go.

SIXTEEN

NO AIR POLLUTION

One of my first attempts to understand God's will was relative to my denominational status as a young minister. I had been saved in a large Baptist church. I love the Baptists, was proud that I was a Baptist, and was quite pleased with the prospect of spending my life as a Baptist minister.

Then I was introduced to the great truth of the baptism of the Holy Spirit. I became extremely interested in this truth because I saw the demonstration of the Spirit-filled life in close friends and relatives. However, I came to understand that my dear Baptist colleagues did not embrace the baptism of the Holy Spirit, and to receive the baptism of the Holy Spirit would mean being isolated from my Baptist fellowship.

Some young men in San Francisco, where I was attending a Bible college, began praying with me each night that I might be filled with the Holy Spirit. These were precious prayer meetings, and I appreciated the concern these young men had that I might be endued with the Pentecostal experience.

Several weeks passed, the prayer meetings progressed, but still I was not filled with the Holy Spirit as the disciples were in the book of Acts.

One night, I arose from my knees, looked at my friends, and said, "Look, fellows, I just don't believe this is the will of God for me. I believe it is God's will that I be a Baptist preacher, and if I receive this baptism of the Holy Spirit, then I could never be a Baptist preacher. No, fellows, I just don't believe this is God's will for me."

One of these friends quickly replied: "Oh, but aren't the Baptists patterned after that great man, John the Baptist?"

I replied, "Yes, John the Baptist is the one from whom the name 'Baptist' was derived."

"Well," my friend went on to say, "the Bible says that John was a man filled with the Holy Ghost. Why don't you just press on and become filled with the Holy Ghost too? If God wants you to be a Baptist preacher, that's all right with us. We don't object. But, brother Don, get filled with the Holy Ghost, and then you can be Don the Baptist!"

That careful spiritual answer really probed my spirit and I did press on to be filled with the Holy Spirit. Oh, praise God! How glad I am that I didn't allow my biases and fears to prevent me from submitting to God's will for my life. Many people have difficulty submitting to the will of God simply because they conceive of it as being something distasteful. Isn't that true? How often have you heard someone say with fatalistic resignation, "Well, it must have been the will of God, so we'll just have to accept it." Even dedicated Christians sometimes say things like, "I intend to do the will of God no matter how much it hurts!"

Now, we all admire such statements of determination and submission. This is good. But do not let yourself think for a moment that God's will is something like bad-tasting medicine that must be "taken" whether we like it or not.

Actually, the opposite is true. You'll never be completely happy until you're in the center of God's will. God's will is good. It is sweet. It is His plan for your life. God always wills that which is best for you and that which will make for your greatest happiness.

But too often, the Devil tempts us to believe that our own will will be better. And the more we think about this, the more our minds are clouded, and we end up making foolish choices which brings nothing but misery.

We need to say, as David said, *"I delight to do thy will, O my God: yea, thy law is within my heart"* (Psalm 40:8). Why did he say that? Because he learned that God's will is good.

We need to think of God's will as Jesus thought of it when he said, *"My meat is to do the will of him that sent me, and to finish his work"* (John 4:34).

Did you get that? God's will isn't bitter medicine; its meat. Like a beef roast. Like a T-bone steak. The performance of God's will is delicious—because it brings peace, joy, and happiness. So don't ever fight His will. Now, I'm convinced that this is why the air is always pure on Praise Avenue. The people who live there are enjoying God's will. Nobody is struggling with the will of God, or complaining about what God wants them to do. You just can't have a better atmosphere than that which comes about when people are enjoying God's will. There's so much air-pollution all around us: there are so many who fight against God's will, fuss about it, rebel against it. But, oh, how refreshing it is to live on an Avenue where people are *"doing the will of God from the heart"* (Ephesians 6:6).

Occasionally, I meet people who just can't decide what the will of God is in some given situation. Now, please forgive me if I oversimplify the matter, but I'm convinced that God will always reveal His will to you if you'll just observe a few simple principles. First and foremost, you must be very careful to keep your motives right. Second, you must be absolutely convinced that God's will is good for you. Third, you must want to know God's will with all of your heart. Fourth, you must spend much time in God's Word. And finally, you must be determined to do God's will when you know it.

When some men consider entering the ministry, for instance, the idea of how much money they will be paid sometimes becomes the determining factor in their decision. But you can see how important it is to keep one's motives right. Although we live in a materialistic world where money provides the answer for many of life's necessities, the pay must always be secondary for a minister of the Gospel. Of course, I certainly believe that ministers should be paid, for the Bible says, *"the Lord ordained that they which preach the gospel should live of the gospel"* (1 Corinthians 9:14). Yet no minister who is truly called by God preaches for money; he preaches for the sheer joy of knowing he is doing God's will for his life.

In my early days, after being filled with the Holy Spirit, a fire was created in my bosom about preaching. God gave me many opportunities. I began preaching at the missions in downtown San Francisco on skid-row. I began preaching on the street corners. I preached at every opportunity I received. Invitations were given me to preach in many black churches in San Francisco. But still that was not enough.

The unquenchable fire burning within my heart demanded that I preach the Gospel everywhere possible. I could say with Paul, *"For though I preach the gospel, I have nothing to glory of: for necessity is laid upon me; yea, woe is unto me, if I preach not the gospel"* (1 Corinthians 9:16)! So every afternoon I took my Bible in hand and walked some blocks to the Geary Street Park in San Francisco, where I would stand in the open air and preach the Gospel.

I would preach on one side of the park where the Jews were assembled, then I would go to the other side of the park and preach to the Gentiles. I felt like Paul, preaching the Gospel *"to the Jew first, and also to the Greek"* (Romans 1:16).

Even though God permitted that I should live for the Gospel for many years now, I have always been aware of the fact that I am really a preacher without regular pay. That is, God called me to preach, and I preach for the delight of obeying His voice, doing His will. With or without pay, I am grateful that God called me to the ministry.

Another incident comes to my mind from those early days of my ministry. The renowned evangelist, William Freeman, came to San Francisco for a city-wide crusade. This five-week's crusade resulted in thousands accepting Christ, and many wonderful miracles of healing were wrought by God's power.

Each night, I, along with the other Bible college students, was busy in the prayer room winning souls to Christ. It was a thrill to be a soul-winner for Christ and to help people come to Jesus. I thank God for the burden He gave me for souls in the very early days of my ministry.

As the weeks progressed, I was encouraged to write an article about the crusade for our college paper, *The Tide*. The famous evangelist liked the article so well that he came to my dormitory to seek me out one night. It was a great honor to have a personal visit from this evangelist who was so highly esteemed by many thousands in San Francisco, including all of the Bible college students.

One night, as William Freeman talked with me, he invited me to travel with him as his personal assistant. I told him that I would pray about it and let him know. Some of my friends found out about the invitation and immediately, I became somewhat of a hero. After all, it was not every day that a college student was invited by such a famous evangelist to travel as his assistant!

Actually, though, the invitation created a real problem for me. I began battling a terrible spirit of pride. Now, I learned long ago that *"God resisteth the proud, but giveth grace unto the humble"* (James 4:6). And I knew that Jesus said, *"Every one that exalteth himself shall be abased; and he that humbleth himself shall be exalted"* (Luke 18:14). And, very frankly, I felt somewhat exalted by the invitation of this evangelist to travel with him in his great city-wide campaigns.

For a few days, I wrestled with this pride and with the personal conflict within my bosom. Should I or should I not accept this invitation? I sincerely desired to travel with Freeman. It was very appealing. I loved to be in great soul-winning crusades. I highly esteemed the ministry of this evangelist. All of it was so very desirable, but yet in my own heart there was the question, "Is this the will of God for my life?"

I was influenced to believe that God's will was something difficult to ascertain, and that only after much painful anxiety and soul-searching could one ever determine what God's will was.

When I look back on it, I realize that many young ministers, Bible college students, and dedicated Christians are in earnest pursuit of God's will. Often, they suffer painful anxiety as I did in those days.

Finally, because of a desire to please God more than anything else, I went to the evangelist and told him that I could not accept his invitation. I asked him to pray for me, that I would understand more about discerning God's will. The evangelist gave me a few pointers from his own experience, and left the issue with me.

After he left San Francisco to go to Seattle for his next campaign, I continued praying about God's will, even though I gave the evangelist my decision that I would not accompany him.

One day, I reached the place of resignation: the old sense of pride over the invitation of a famous evangelist, any feeling of being superior to my fellow students, or any other selfish attitude—all of this was melted away by the love of Jesus. I just submitted myself and said, "Lord, not my will, but Thine be done."

Interestingly enough, it was not long before I received a long distance telephone call from Freeman, and I knew the matter was settled. I accepted the invitation, and that was the beginning of a most exciting adventure in my ministry for Jesus.

Now, after many years of following God's will in various kinds of ministries, I can say that my greatest satisfaction in life has been gained in doing what I knew God wanted me to do.

God's will is like a breath of fresh air pure, clean, and exhilarating. I don't know of anything that will keep you praising like fulfilling God's perfect plan for your life, whatever it is.

SEVENTEEN

SOCIAL SECURITY

Aminister from Tennessee named Stevens was here in Canada with his wife conducting special meetings in a large church. They had left their children in the care of the grandparents in Tennessee.

Brother Stevens was not only winning many people to Jesus, but was being used of God to cast out demons in Jesus' name. Because of his success in this area, the Devil became infuriated and began tormenting Brother Stevens with the thought that he was going to kill the Stevens' children.

Brother Stevens said, "Devil, you're a liar! You cannot kill my children."

To this, the Devil seemed to say, "Oh, yes, I can, for I have put rabies upon the foxes in the woods adjoining your property." Immediately, Brother Stevens remembered the reports of friends who had seen foxes roaming on his land before he left Tennessee.

In simple childlike faith, Brother Stevens gathered together three other believers. Together they agreed in prayer, and by faith they drew a blood-line of protection around the Stevens' property. After all, their property belonged to Jesus. So did they. And so did their children. They were "purchased" by the blood of Jesus. So they felt confident that Jesus' blood-line would be all the security they needed.

A week later, Brother Stevens received a letter from his brother back in Tennessee. He said, "Today I was out walking. I walked around the edge of your property. Lying on the boundary of your land I found five dead foxes. We had the heads examined and found they were all rabid."

The foxes dropped dead when they tried to cross the blood-line! Truly, there is supernatural security in the precious blood of Jesus!

When I heard this story, I decided to draw a bloodline by faith around our evangelistic offices west of Cloverdale, British Columbia. We had serious break-ins that devastated our offices. As I surveyed the destruction of these satanically-inspired thieves, I called my wife and family together. By faith, we drew a blood-line around our offices. That was in 1969. We've never had a break-in at our offices since. Hallelujah! We're secure!

I've challenged hundreds of Christians to draw a blood-line, by faith, around their property. The results have been amazing. I really believe in the power of the blood of Jesus. I'm convinced that God honors our childlike faith in that blood.

Recently, my favorite suit, my shirt and tie were stolen from my hotel room while we were conducting special meetings. And a short time later, when my daughter Judy was participating at "Jesus '74" in Pennsylvania, robbers broke into the room that she and Andrae Crouch's sister were sharing and stole $300.

After that, we enlarged the extent of our blood-line to include hotel rooms! Now we don't feel insecure in the least. We just go on our way praising God.

Praise Avenue is the most secure place in the world. What makes it so? The blood of Jesus. We've been bought by His precious blood. We're His property. And because we're His, He looks after us and keeps us in the hollow of His hand.

Talk about social security! Never has anyone been more socially secure then when he trusts in the blood of Jesus, and opens his mouth in praises to the Most High God.

There is an interesting verse in Proverbs 30:26 which says, *"The conies are but a feeble folk, yet make they their houses in the rocks."* And what is a coney? Why, a coney is a lovable, furry little animal something like a rabbit, only it has short ears, short legs, and no tail.

Now the writer of the Proverbs says that the conies are but a feeble folk. Such helpless little things! And so timid, too! Yet they make their houses in the rocks. They burrow into the cracks and hollows of rocky cliffs and caves, and find security there.

So don't pity the poor, helpless coney. He has found something that many a man and woman wish they could find. Security! Protection from the perils of life! A shelter in the time of storm! For while the thunder cracks and rocks the countryside, and while the lightning rips across the sky, and while the wind shrieks and howls, the coney is safe.

We can take a lesson from this little fellow. He scurries into his hole in the rock, and as he looks around at his rocky shelter, I can almost hear him saying, "I am weak, but thou art strong." And he huddles up close to the rock, and enjoys the security of his little nest.

And then I think of the many Christians on Praise Avenue who have found their security in God. They're even more secure than the coney. Yet there are always certain other people who misunderstand these secure Christians and say, "My, he surely is a strong Christian."

But, no—there is no such thing as a strong Christian—only as he is strong in the Lord and in the power of His might. A Christian, in himself, is as weak and exposed to peril as a coney. And I shudder to think what would become of our Christian lives if God left us to ourselves. We couldn't live the Christian life. We'd give into temptation. We'd go back to our sins. There just isn't enough spiritual strength in any of us to live as a Christian should.

But, thank God, there is a place of shelter. God's promises stand like giant walls of rock. *"Be not afraid,"* He says to us, *"for the Lord thy God is with thee"* (Joshua 1:9). And I believe that, don't you? I have found in God and His Word a supernatural strength which I never believed possible. As I have trusted in Jesus, I have found myself, like David in the Cave of Adullam, safe from every attack of the enemy.

Let me say that name again: Jesus! Rock of Ages! Shelter in the time of storm! Jesus! The Rock in a weary land. And, my friends, a long time ago when burdened by sin, I fled to the cleft of the Rock, and found safety and security.

This is the greatest security there is. No king in his fortress is more secure than the coney in the rocks. No man of state with secret service men surrounding him is as well protected as the little dweller in the mountain clefts. In Jesus, the weak are strong and the defenseless are safe. As long as you're trusting in His blood, there's nothing to fear.

Do you want to draw a blood-line by faith around yourself and your property? Then affirm these power-packed words: "In the name of Jesus, I draw a bloodline by faith around myself, my property, my home, my car, my clothes, and my possessions. I draw a bloodline by faith, knowing there is power, wonder-working power, in the blood of Jesus." Neither Satan, nor any of his cohorts, can cross such a blood-line!

Such confidence in the effectiveness of the blood of Jesus is Bible-based. The Word of God says, *"Forasmuch as ye know that you were not redeemed with corruptible things, as silver and gold, from your vain conversation received by tradition from your fathers; but with the precious blood of Christ, as of a lamb without blemish and without spot"* (1 Peter 1:18–19).

As a believer, you have a right to the protection of His shed blood. And with that protection, you're perfectly secure on Praise Avenue.

EIGHTEEN

JUST KIDS

A farmer was showing a friend around his beautiful farm. The friend was greatly impressed by the well-kept buildings, white fences, and lush, green fields. But the thing that impressed him most of all was the splendid sheep he saw in the farmer's well-watered pastures.

"What beautiful sheep!" he exclaimed. "I've never seen nicer sheep anywhere!"

"Yep," the farmer grinned, "they're about the most perfect specimens you'll find anywhere."

"But, tell me," the visitor inquired, "how did you ever succeed in raising such a magnificent flock like this?"

"It's easy," the farmer replied. "I just take good care of the lambs."

I hope that story speaks to you the way it speaks to me. If you're a parent on Praise Avenue and have children, I'm sure you understand the importance of taking good care of the "lambs." The kids must learn to praise God, too. Praise Avenue ought to be full of lively children who know how to say "Thank You, Jesus!" and "Hallelujah!" Curly-headed girls swinging in the backyards ought to enjoy singing lively praise-songs. Freckle-faced boys on Praise Avenue's baseball lot ought to say "Praise the Lord" when they slam a homer. This praise life isn't just for old folks—the sheep. No, the lambs need to be taught to praise God. How sad it would be if they grew up not knowing how to praise.

Now, obviously, children aren't going to learn how to praise the Lord if it isn't perfectly natural at home. If you're a praising parent, you'll have praising children. We need to spend much time with our children, indoctrinating them in the things of God, praying and praising with them, and helping them to memorize the Scriptures.

Do you remember what Jesus said to Peter in John 21:15? He said, *"Feed my lambs."* Since Jesus is the Chief Shepherd, He knows the importance of properly feeding and nurturing the lambs. We spend much time teaching our children how to walk, talk, and eat. But how are we doing in spiritual things? Are you teaching your lambs to walk in the ways of the Lord? To talk praise? To "eat" the Word?

Once you've taught your children to be good residents of Praise Avenue, you'll sometimes be surprised how God uses them to minister to your own heart. Some years ago, my wife and I, with our little boy, Michael, were returning from a special minister's gathering. We were discussing how it seemed that there was a general tendency to conform to each other among the ministers, and that so many were bound by traditions. We were assuring ourselves that we certainly didn't want a ministry that was a copy of someone else's.

Suddenly, our little Michael turned to me with real fervor and said, "Daddy, be like Jesus!"

It struck a real note in my heart, as he again repeated it, while looking right in my face: "Daddy, be like Jesus!"

If Michael, the archangel, spoke those words, they would not have had more of an impact. I knew that the Bible said that God ordained strength out of the mouths of babes. (See Psalm 8:2.) I knew those words had real significance, and my wife and I were confident that the Lord was speaking to my heart. The message was loud and clear: "Daddy, be like Jesus!"

Another unforgettable time was when Judy was four years old. She overheard my wife and I discuss some crucial financial problems.

In our family prayer that evening, I asked each of our children to pray "around the circle." Michael prayed first and then Jeanne. When it came Judy's time, she worded her fervent prayer as follows: "Lord, please give us strong food to eat; and Lord, give us strong clothes to wear; and dear Lord, give us bills to pay."

I was amazed for a few moments as I thought of her prayer. It was amusing, but so deeply earnest from her little heart that I dared not laugh. And I was quite sure the dear Lord understood her petition even better than I.

Often, when we are faced with great financial obligations, I remember Judy's prayer and take courage that the Lord does understand our needs. And if we have bills that He has sent, then He will supply the money to pay them. So I've begun to see that I can praise God even for my bills!

Some of the greatest experiences of my Christian life have come in being a father. I'm the proud and happy father of five children. It has been one of the deepest and most delightful satisfactions in life—to be the father of these children.

I love to play with my children. We have ball games together. We enjoy each other's company. And we like to work together.

But among the sweetest and most endearing times of my life have been our prayer-times together. We have endeavored to make our family worship very important. We believe it should be made so pleasant as to be looked forward to with gladness, even by the youngest children. If care is not given here, family worship can be made tedious, monotonous, or burdensome. To make it dull or irksome is treason to true worship.

One morning at an early hour, I was on my knees in the kitchen trying to "pray through." But there was no victory, joy, nor blessing for me in that time of prayer.

Then my little son, Michael, just learning how to walk and talk, found me there in the kitchen. He quietly snuggled up beside me, put his baby arms around my neck and said, "Daddy, I'm thirsty. I want a drink of water."

Quickly, I arose and got him a glass of water to quench his thirst. Then I embraced him tenderly, and had a captivating time of fellowship with him.

Since it was still early, he wanted to go back to bed. As I carried him through the house to his bedroom, I was suddenly enchanted by the rapturous knowledge that I was a father, and this was my own little boy.

I returned to the kitchen to resume my prayer-time. It still seemed unattractive and dull. But then, so lovingly, so assuringly, the blessed Holy Spirit spoke these words to my heart:

> *What man is there of you, whom if his son ask bread, will he give him a stone? Or if he ask a fish, will he give him a serpent? If ye then, being evil, know how to give good gifts unto your children, how much more shall your Father which is in heaven give good things to them that ask him?*
>
> (Matthew 7:9–11)

I pondered these words. They warmed my heart and challenged me. I, Don Gossett, was a father. I knew how to give good gifts to my children. When I was out in evangelistic crusades away from my wife and children, I would usually plan to take some little gifts to them. I would always select their gifts with thought and care.

But Jesus said so clearly, "How *much more* shall your Father which is in heaven give good things to them that ask him?"

I began to see that I, too, am just one of God's "kids" on the Avenue. And my Father is looking after me, just as I am looking after my children. And if I delight to give good gifts to my children, how much more does my Father in heaven desire to give good things to them (that included me) that ask Him!

Suddenly, the light had shone from heaven! The Holy Spirit illuminated my mind and heart. Never again would I pray with the feeling that my Father didn't care. Never again would I let myself think I was unworthy. No! I was His child, dear unto Him. He redeemed me through the blood of Jesus Christ, His Son and my Savior.

Every provision had already been made for me to have a joyful prayer life. The door to the throne room was open. In Hebrews 4:16, he said, *"Let us therefore come boldly unto the throne of grace, that we may obtain mercy, and find grace to help in time of need."* Hallelujah! Jesus made a way so that I could fellowship with the Father in the throne room.

I could lovingly look up to Him, and say, "My Father." And I could hear Him say in my innermost being, "My child."

Never again would I be dull in His presence. I knew He loved me far more than I could ever love my own children.

Praise God! This was liberating morning for my prayer life. No longer would I go through "vain repetitions." Now I could pray with great freedom and assurance. The Father, who is the author of every good and perfect gift, would freely give to me as I ask Him.

And all of this came about when God let me see the truth about His concern for me.

My love for our children was but a microscopic example of the kind of love God has for all of His "kids" on Praise Avenue.

Big "kids"—and little "kids"—they're all objects of His care.

NINETEEN

HERE'S WHAT THEY SAY

Praise Avenue is the longest avenue in the world. In fact, everywhere I've gone, all around the world, I've met residents of the Avenue. It's been a fascinating avocation to collect the testimonies of this wonderful multitude of praisers, and I'd like to take this final chapter to pass along just a few of their testimonies about the miracle-working power of praise.

———

First, I'd like to tell you about a man whom I'll call "Ronald," from Springfield, Oregon. Unfortunately, I can't remember his real name.

I had been ministering at the First Assembly of God Church in Springfield. On a particular Sunday, I had been preaching for three weeks; then came the Sunday night service. The Holy Spirit led me to speak on the subject of praise. After preaching about this truth and leading the people into the glorious life of praise, I closed the service. But no sooner had I said the last "Amen" that Ronald approached me on the platform.

"Brother Gossett," he said, "you have preached about the power of praise. I'm a living testimony of how the Lord responds to praise. Just one year ago, I was dying in the hospital. I was in intensive care with emphysema. The doctors told my family that I had only five minutes to live. When I realized I had only five minutes more to live, I decided to devote those five minutes to praising my Lord for all the mercies and blessings I had known in my lifetime.

Ronald went on, "As I began to praise the Lord, the Holy Spirit responded and ministered a miracle in my life. Instead of my lungs closing up with the emphysema, the process was reversed. The Lord inhabited my praises; His response opened up my lungs and I began being made whole from that time on. In a few days, I was released from the hospital, made completely well by the power of the Lord."

Isn't that wonderful? Ron's testimony reminds us that the Lord still inhabits our praises and that His miracles are still manifested when we lavish loving praises upon Him.

———

The more I study the Word of God, and the more I hear the testimonies of the Lord's people, the more I am convinced that praise is the key. Praise is the key to all things pertaining to both life and godliness. Praise is the key to the Holy Spirit baptism. Praise is the key to the presence of God.

Mr. and Mrs. Perry Cowger of Burnaby, British Columbia, were on a holiday north of Fort St. John, B.C. While traveling many miles from where anyone lived, they stopped beside a river for a picnic. When they were ready to continue their journey, they could not find their car keys. In desperation, they searched all over the car and around the area where they had their picnic. But their search was fruitless.

Brother Cowger shares their dilemma: "We looked everywhere possible. No keys were to be found! We prayed fervently, but it seemed there was no answer to our prayers."

Suddenly Mrs. Cowger thought of a possible solution for their problem. "Brother Gossett tells us to 'praise the Lord anyhow!'"

she stated. "Let's praise the Lord right here in these desperate circumstances and see what happens."

Brother and Sister Cowger lifted their hands and voices and
praised the Lord right out there in their place of isolation, many
miles from anyone and anywhere.

Brother Cowger testifies, "When we began praising the Lord,
we glanced at a certain spot on the ground, and there were the
keys!"

Beloved, when you begin praising the Lord, you have the keys.
You have the keys to every spiritual blessing in heavenly places in
Christ Jesus. You have the keys to divine healing and health. You
have the keys to God's deliverance from any oppression.

———

There is something of which I am very sure: when you start
praising Jesus, things happen. Maybe not always spectacular
things, nor things you can see with your eyes or feel with your
emotions—but in the realm of the Holy Spirit, things happen in
your life.

Sometimes the manifestation of praise permeates the physical
body and produces notable results. Such is the testimony of Mr.
George C. McComber of Delta, British Columbia.

"On a short holiday last month," George says, "I developed a
terrific headache. Several months earlier, I had been prayed over
because of these headaches. As a result of that prayer, I decided I
didn't need my pills any longer, so I threw them away. But by the
time I got home, my head was throbbing with pain. I prayed and
told the Lord I didn't want to buy any more pills—but I had to do
something. Reluctantly, my family and I drove up the hill to the
pharmacy. Then I remembered what you said about praise, and I
started praising Jesus.

"No sooner had I started praising when I noticed that the throbbing faded. As the car climbed the hill, I kept praising Jesus, wondering if the throbbing would suddenly start up again. By the time we reached the top of the hill, my family and I were all shouting praises to Jesus. The headache never returned and I never bought more pills. I believe this particular headache was a direct challenge for me to go directly to the Lord in praise. This incident brought me to a greater maturity and faith. I haven't had any headaches since."

It's the Holy Spirit Who performs such miracles in our lives today. He is so zealous for Jesus to be exalted, glorified, and praised that He just manifests Himself in supernatural ways when a believer praises Jesus.

It's interesting to me that Brother McComber said he already started up the hill to the pharmacy. That climb signified a defeat in his faith walk. But he turned that journey of defeat into one of triumph, simply by praise!

There's no doubt about it: when you praise Jesus, things happen!

What is the hill you're facing? Are you battling certain defeat? You can't do anything better than praising Jesus right where you are.

When should you praise Him? Just now, stop what you're doing, lift up your heart and hands and voice and begin to love and praise the Lord Jesus Christ. He is deserving of all your praise.

Did you ever take a "praise-walk?" Miss Mattie Eskridge of Los Angeles, California, relates this experience:

"I thank the Lord for your instructions about praise. When I first started praising the Lord, I was plagued with many fears. Unbeknown to me, my mother, who had been sick, had to go to the hospital again. After I was informed that she was in the hospital, I grew very depressed. I went home that evening feeling very low, and I sat down and poured my heart out to the Lord. He brought to my remembrance one of your teachings about praise. You had suggested that we walk through the house with our hands raised, praising the Lord. I did this, and the Lord brought a wonderful calmness over me, and He let me know that He was going to bring mother back home well.

"And, indeed, the Lord brought my mother back home, and He is steadily healing her body. Praise lifts our minds and eyes off circumstances and places them on the promises of God."

Have you ever taken a praise-walk through your home? Why not do so now? Walk through every room, hallway, and area of your home. Fill it with the praises of the Lord. I assure you there will be results: God will inhabit that home mightily with His presence!

When I think about the fall of Jericho, I am reminded of the people of God marching around the walls of that city with their hearts full of praise to the Lord. God was pleased with their praise-walk and manifested His supernatural power. Today or tonight—soon—have a praise-walk through your home. Raise your hands as you praise Him. I've discovered this to be one of the sweet secrets of preparation for spiritual activity—to walk and praise.

————

Mrs. Earle Leavitt of St. George, New Brunswick, became so delighted with her life of praise that she started "praise classes" in her home. In a recent letter, Mrs. Leavitt shared another letter with me that was sent by one of her "pupils." I think the letter is worth sharing:

This is a dynamic subject: the power of praise. It seems that the Lord answers from the secret place of thunder when you praise Him.

By praising Him, you will receive honey out of the rock, satisfying your soul, giving you a healthy body! Praise will drive out infirm spirits and loosen the bones!

Heart trouble will not overcome you, and should you have it, it will leave you as you praise the Lord continually. Praise will make your heart happy and your body joyful and healthful. Your eyes will sparkle and your vision will be plainer! By eating lightly and by praising Him, your well-being will intensify even more. Also, the dull ear shall hear sharply! Even your complexion—your hair and your lips—will take on a beautiful glow!

Praising the Lord in intervals will drive back all demon powers from you, and you'll have rest and peace. By praising Him often, you'll be covered with a bright shekinah glory; whether you can see it all the time or not, you'll begin feeling it by the glory of His presence. Demons cannot break through this covering as long as you praise the Lord in confidence!

Praising the Lord renews youthfulness and strength, gives faith, and allows the Holy Spirit to speak. Praise exalts the Most High and allows His Spirit to flow through you, providing a ministry for each of us as the Spirit wills it in our own lives.

Also, prosperity is as close as one's lips; if you continually praise the Lord, no matter what confronts you, you will win! A kingly anointing will ever be present.

After David wrote the Psalms, he was still praising the Lord at the end of them. The very last verse of those Psalms reads "Let everything that hath *breath praise the Lord. Praise ye the Lord"* (Psalm 150:6). A person who has the high praises of God in his mouth will receive knowledge and wisdom, guiding him in his daily affairs and giving him many spiritual insights into life!

The one who humbles himself and praises the Lord will be anointed above his brethren. He shall feel and walk like a king. Spiritually speaking, the ground will sing under him and a cloud of love will engulf him! He will feel the Lord's hand on his back and on his head, and he shall be covered by the Most High!

Why is there such power in praise? Because that it is the reason we were created: to praise the Lord of Hosts. The Lord did not create us merely to continually ask for things that are secondary; we were made to praise Him! When we get into the rhythm of praise, we will feel the sweetness of His presence, and He will reveal the most secret things to us.

These are some of the most beautiful words on praise I've ever read. There's absolutely no limit to what we can accomplish when we praise God in every situation.

———

Mrs. Irma Dons of Red Deer, Alberta, exercised the language of faith and received a wonderful miracle. She writes, "Praise the Lord! I too want to share the truth that there is victory in praise. I suffered with bronchitis, then asthma, for thirty-two years in all. I tried all the usual medication, which brought only temporary relief; a cure seemed out of the question.

"Then I went to Calgary for your meetings. I was very sick at the time and wondered if I could take the ninety-mile drive to Calgary. But I went by faith, praising the Lord.

"I'll never forget what the Lord did for me that day. As you laid your hands on me and started praying, you told me to start praising the Lord and thanking Him. So I did. Praise the Lord, the Lord healed me of my asthma, double pneumonia, and opened up some collapsed lobes in my lungs! Again, I say, Praise the Lord! I've continued praising the Lord every day, and I've had no medication since that beautiful day. Hallelujah!"

You see, praise is the language of faith. Faith is expressed not only by confession of the Word, but also by praising the Lord. Public praise, especially, is most effective. The faith that dares to praise God in the face of trying circumstances, even when others are listening, is the faith that brings results.

———

There are two times to praise the Lord: (1) When you feel like praising the Lord; and (2) when you don't feel like praising the Lord.

It's just that simple. Indeed, the Lord is to be praised when you feel joy in your soul, ecstasy of spirit, and hilarity because of His presence and His victories. But praise is especially for those times when you don't feel like it. Miss Charlotte Walther of Jefferson City, Missouri, discovered this truth:

> I had a new job with greater responsibilities, and it seemed impossible for me to learn this new job and be able to feel that I was doing it adequately. Well, one night, I decided to quit begging God to remove the difficult situation, and to try very hard not to complain, but rather praise the Lord anyhow.
>
> So I went down the row of machines in the plastics department, doing my inspection. It seemed that everything went wrong. I was behind in my inspection, and late for everything. As more things piled up, I started laughing!

I praised the Lord and said, "Lord, I can't help but laugh. The situation is so impossible, it's funny!"

Even though I laughed and praised Him, the situation did not change, believe me. Instead, it seemed to grow even worse, if that's possible. But nevertheless, I found a new strength, courage, and release in my Spirit to meet the challenge. Since then, the job is still not any less demanding, but I have found even more strength and courage than before. Indeed, the joy of the Lord is my strength. So I'm learning to praise Him daily, regardless of the situation.

By far, the hardest thing for me to praise the Lord for was loneliness. I always wanted to be married, and I kept asking, "Why not, Lord?" I grew discontented, bitter, cynical, and disenchanted with my life in Christ.

One day at home, I was complaining in my usual way, when it occurred to me that I should praise the Lord in spite of it all. The very moment I opened my mouth and said, "Praise you, Jesus, in spite of my not having a home and family," I felt immediate release in my Spirit and joy started flowing. I never before thought to praise God in spite of it all. It works, and I'm thrilled! Praise His lovely name! It's now with joy that I'm learning to be content in whatever situation the Lord puts me in. It's a joy to share this testimony with you.

———

Through the years, I have experienced healing after healing through the power of praising the Lord. I have encouraged many people to praise their way to healing. As people have continually praised and blessed God, healing virtue has flowed in and the Lord has made them whole. Sometimes it's necessary to hold yourself steady by praise until the healing is fully manifested, but surely the Lord watches over His Word to perform it.

Charles J. Martz of Brooklyn, New York, wrote me this letter:

> I was sixty-one years old when Jesus saved me. I praise Him for His great love. Then His Holy Spirit led me into praise and thanksgiving. He filled my cup to overflowing, with many more blessings than I deserve. Then he put the icing on the cake with the baptism of the Holy Ghost. I am now seventy years young, and it seems as time passes that I get more fired up for the Lord Jesus.
>
> Some time ago, I was stricken with severe sciatica pain in my right leg and hip. Walking was a jaw-gritting experience. But by praising God and repeating, "Thank you, Jesus," constantly for thirty-six hours, I was healed. Praise our mighty God!
>
> If you need healing for your body, praise the Lord, saying, "Thank You, Jesus; by Thy stripes I am healed." Repeat that. Keep on praising the Lord. I want to encourage you to expect a complete manifestation of healing as you continue praising Him.

———

One of the most important facts to keep in mind about praise is that we must persevere against adverse feelings. In any given day, a hundred and one negative feelings can come across our minds and spirits. Sometimes, this is caused by others' words and actions toward us. At other times, there are those unexplainable "blank feelings," plus feelings of depression, heaviness of heart, and dark clouds hanging over us. Through it all, we must praise the Lord and rout these troublesome feelings.

Mrs. Mary Slagel of Tacoma, Washington, shares her experience along this line:

> The most outstanding result of praise that we've experienced happened when my husband and I were pastors of

the Indian Revival Centre here. I lodged anyone who came along, since we had a four-bedroom house and a basement with beds in it. There was much cooking to do and rooms to keep tidy. One day, we sat down to eat and my legs ached so badly I almost cried. I was returning thanks for the food and said, 'Oh, I thank and praise You, Jesus, for every ache and pain.'

The Spirit of the Lord came down and swept over me from my head to my heels, like warm oil all over me. Every ache and pain left, and, oh, the joy that filled my soul! I've had many sorrows and heartaches all my Christian life. But they have been the means of making Jesus so real to me. I love Him so very, very much.

———

Mrs. B. Maser of Edmonton, Alberta, adds her testimony:

Brother Gossett, it's wonderful to live the praise life. I had a bad pain in my lower back and left leg all the way down to my ankle. At times, I could not stand on my feet to do my work—and when I did stand, it was never any longer than ten or fifteen minutes. I had to sit down or lie down to relieve the pain. I had this pain for about five or six years. Last winter especially was very bad.

In the spring, I sent a prayer request to you for the pain in my leg and back, and also was prayed for in our church. Then I began praising the Lord, saying, "Thank You, Lord Jesus; through Your stripes I am healed." The next day, after I praised the Lord again for my healing, I was able to do my work. Later that week, it dawned on me that I had been able to work all week long without any more pain. It was so wonderful; it felt as if I had a new back and leg. Praise the Lord Jesus that by His stripes I am healed!

And so they continue coming—multiplied reports of the power of praise. My files are full of such testimonials. As I read these letters, one thing is very obvious: every resident of Praise Avenue is convinced that praise really works.

ABOUT THE AUTHOR

For more than fifty years, Don Gossett has been serving the Lord through full-time ministry. Born again at the age of twelve, Don answered his call to the ministry just five years later, beginning by reaching out to his unsaved family members. In March 1948, Don overcame his longtime fear of public speaking and began his ministry in earnest, preaching for two country Baptist churches in Oklahoma.

Blessed with the gift of writing, Don became editor of the Bible College magazine in San Francisco; afterward, he was invited to become editor of an international magazine. Following this, he served as editor of T. L. Osborn's *Faith Digest*, a magazine that reached over 600,000 homes each month.

Don has penned many works, particularly ones on the power of the spoken word and praise. His writings have been translated into almost twenty languages and have exceeded twenty-five million in worldwide distribution. Additionally, Don has recorded scores of audio series. His daily radio broadcast, launched in 1961, has been released into eighty-nine nations worldwide.

Don raised five children with his first wife, Joyce, who died in 1991. In 1995, Don found lifelong love again and married Debra, an anointed teacher of the Word. They have ministered worldwide and have lived in British Columbia, Canada, and in Blaine, Washington State.

In September 2009, Don and Debra (also an ordained minister) founded a new church in Vancouver, British Columbia, where they continue to serve as pastors. The International Community Church truly is an international body of believers with members from many nations sharing a vision: to bring the saving, healing, and restoring power of Jesus to the community, locally and abroad.